TANTRA

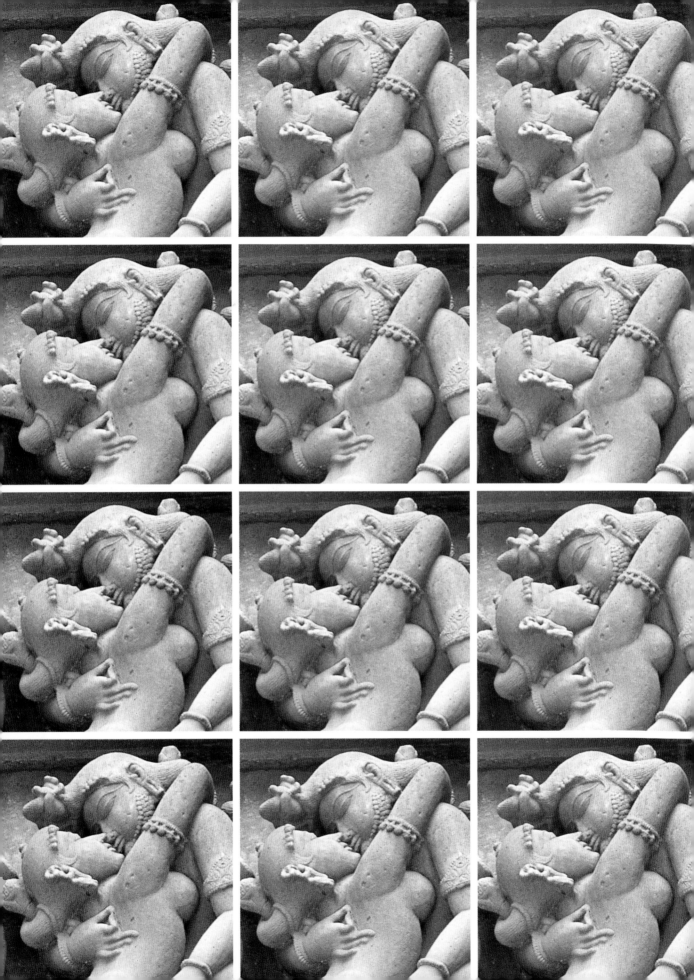

TANTRA

the way of acceptance

OSHO

An Ixos Press Book

First published in 2005

Book © Ixos Press, a division of the Bridgewater Book Company
Text © 2005 Osho International Foundation, Switzerland. www.osho.com

ISBN: 0-681-06902-3

Created and produced by

Ixos Press
The Old Candlemakers
West Street
Lewes
East Sussex
BN7 2NZ
UK

Creative Director: Peter Bridgewater
Art Director: Sarah Howerd
Commissioning Editor: Mark Truman
Designer: Alistair Plumb

Printed in China

The text material in this book is selected from various discourses by Osho
given to a live audience over a period of more than thirty years. All of
the Osho discourses have been published in full as books, and are also
available as original audio recordings. Audio recordings and the complete
text archive can be found via the on-line OSHO Library at www.osho.com

OSHO is a registered trademark of Osho International Foundation, used
with permission/license.

Picture acknowledgments
The publishers would like to thank the Osho International Foundation for
permission to reproduce the images on pp. 1, 2, 9, 11T, 11B, 13, 15, 16,
19, 20, 23, 26, 27, 28, 30, 32, 37, 39, 41, 48L, 48R, 49, 51T, 51M, 51B, 53,
55L, 55R, 57, 59, 60, 63, 65T, 65BL, 65BR, 66, 67, 69L, 69TR, 69BR, 72,
75, 76T, 76B, 79, 81, 82, 85, 87, 89TL, 89TR, 89BL, 89BR, 90L, 90R, 91,
93, 103, 104L, 104R, 106L, 106R, 107, 109, 110, 113, 115, 117L, 117R,
118T, 118B, 121T, 121B, 123, 124, 125, 126L, 126R, 129, 131, 133, 134T,
134B, 135, 137T, 137M, 139TL, 139TR, 139BL, 140, 143T, 143M, 143B,
with special thanks to Atmo Sharna for the images on pages 34T, 34M,
34B, 95T, 95B, 97L, 97R, 99T, 99BL, 99BR, 100L, 100R, 101L, 101R.

The publishers would also like to thank Corbis Images/Jose Luis Pelaez,
Inc., for permission to reproduce the image on p. 71 and Corbis
Images/Larry Williams for permission to reproduce the image on p. 73.

contents

introduction

*The most basic thing about Tantra is this—and it is radical,
revolutionary, rebellious—the basic principle of Tantra is that the
world is not divided into the lower and the higher, but that it is one
piece. The higher and the lower are holding hands. The higher
contains the lower, and the lower contains the higher. The higher is
hidden in the lower—so the lower has not to be denied, has not to
be condemned, has not to be destroyed or killed. The lower has to
be transformed. The lower has to be allowed to move upward and
in that way the lower* becomes *the higher.*

Another way of saying it is that there is no unbridgeable gap between the Devil and God—the Devil is carrying God deep down in his heart. Once that heart starts functioning, the Devil becomes God. In fact, the word *devil* comes from the same root as the word *divine*; it is the divine not yet evolved, that's all. Not that the Devil is against the divine, not that the Devil is trying to destroy the divine—in fact, the Devil is trying to *find* the divine. The Devil is on the way to the divine; it is not the enemy, it is a seed. The divine is the tree fully in bloom, and the Devil is the seed—but the tree is hidden in the seed. T̶̶̶̶̶̶̶̶̶̶gainst the tree; in fact, the tree cannot exist if the ̶̶̶̶̶̶̶̶̶̶'s not against the seed—they are in deep frien̶̶̶̶̶̶̶

Po̶̶̶̶̶̶̶̶ same energy. So are life and death—and so is e̶̶̶̶̶̶̶̶̶̶̶ate, sex and superconsciousness. Tantra says, N̶̶̶̶̶̶̶̶̶̶le of condemnation is destructive. By condemn̶̶̶̶̶̶̶e possibilities that would have become available t̶̶̶̶̶̶̶̶̶̶r to evolve. Don't condemn the mud, because the̶̶̶̶̶̶̶̶mud to produce the lotus. Of course, the mud is ̶̶̶̶̶̶̶̶eative person will help the mud to release its lot̶̶̶̶

The Tantra ̶̶̶̶̶̶̶̶̶̶̶̶ularly for the present moment in human history, ̶̶̶̶̶̶̶̶̶̶g is striving to be born; a new consciousness is ̶̶̶̶̶̶̶̶̶̶is going to be that of Tantra because dualistic ̶̶̶̶̶̶̶̶̶̶r over the human mind. For centuries, these du̶̶̶̶̶̶̶̶̶̶beings and made them feel guilty. They have no̶̶̶̶̶̶̶̶̶̶them prisoners. They have not made people ha̶̶̶̶̶̶̶̶̶̶m miserable. They have condemned everything̶̶̶̶̶̶̶̶̶̶emned *everything*—from relationship to friendshi̶̶̶̶̶̶̶̶̶̶ondemned, the mind is condemned. They have n̶̶̶̶̶̶̶̶̶̶; they have taken away everything, and you are lef̶̶̶̶̶̶̶̶̶̶

This state cannot be toler̶̶̶̶̶̶̶̶̶.̶ Tantra can give you a new perspective.

tantra: the meeting of
earth and sky

Have you watched a tree growing—how it gropes and grows—what method does it follow? From the seed comes the sprout, and then slowly, slowly, it starts rising upward. It comes from deep down in the earth, and then it starts rising into the sky, from root to trunk and branch and leaf and flower and fruit.... This is what happens with your tree of life, too.

There is no distinction between the sacred and the profane.

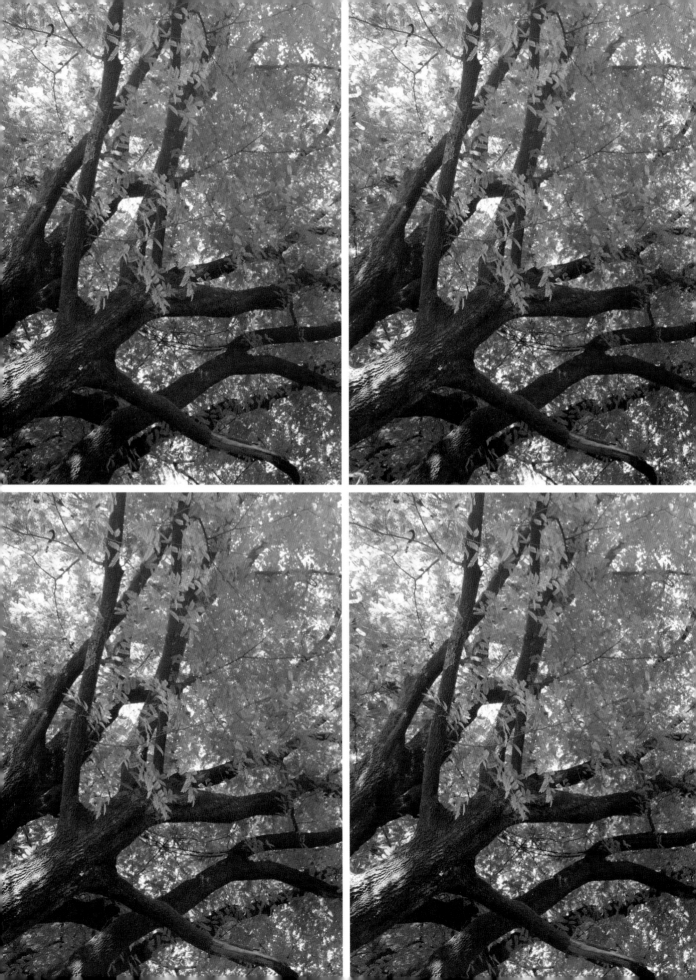

the serpent is the savior

Sex is as sacred as Samadhi. The lowest and the highest are part of one continuum. The lowest rung is as much part of the ladder as the highest rung; they are nowhere divided. If you deny the lower, you will never be able to reach to the higher.

Sex is nothing to feel guilty about; it is your life. It is where you are—how can you avoid it? If you avoid it, you will be inauthentic, untrue. If you avoid it or repress it, you will not be able to move upward because your energy will be repressed through it.

When your sexuality starts moving, that's a good sign. It shows that you have been contacted, that something has stirred in you, that something has become a movement in you: you are no longer a stagnant pool—you have started flowing toward the ocean.

Certainly, the ocean is far away. It will come at the very end. But if you stop this small muddy pool from flowing, you will never reach the ocean. I know the mud of it, but it has to be accepted. You have to start flowing!

The serpent and the savior are not two—they are one. In fact, there is an ancient tradition that says that after God created Adam and Eve and told them they should not go to the Tree of Knowledge and they should not eat the fruit of it—then God became the serpent. He coiled himself around the tree and seduced Eve to eat the fruit of the tree. God himself became the serpent!

I love this story. Some Christians will be shocked. But only God can do such a thing—nobody else. From where can the serpent come? And without God's help, how can the serpent convince Eve? In fact, the whole thing was decided beforehand: God wanted man to go astray, because only by going astray does one become mature. God wanted man to commit sin, because only through sin does one someday arrive at sainthood. There is no other way.

That's why God said, "Don't eat the fruit of this tree!" This is simple psychology. What Christians say, if they are right, means that God is not even as much a psychologist as Sigmund Freud. It is simple psychology that if you prohibit somebody from something, that something becomes more attractive, more magnetic. If you say, "Don't do this!" you can be sure it will be done. Every parent knows this, and God is the ultimate parent. Will he not know it?

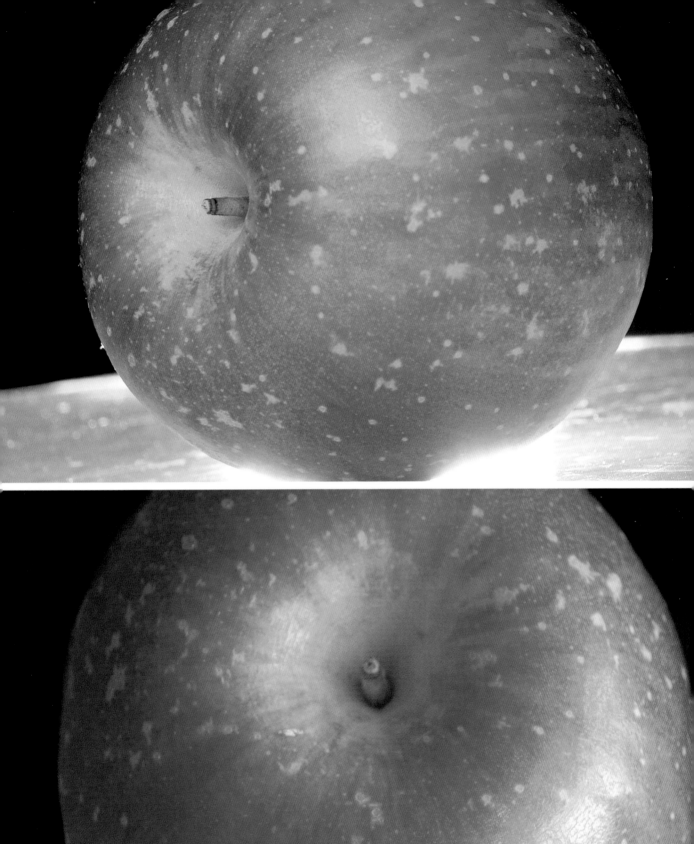

> *In the East, the serpent has never been in the service of the Devil; it has always been in the service of God.*

There is a story:

Freud had gone to a garden park with his wife and child, and they walked around in the beautiful spring evening. They were paying no mind to the child when suddenly it was time for closing. The bell began to ring and everybody was supposed to leave. Freud's wife said, "But where is our child? He has disappeared!" And it was a big park.

Freud said, "Tell me only one thing: did you prohibit him from going anywhere?"

And she said, "Yes, I told him not to go near the fountain."

Then he said, "Let's go. If my insight is true, he will be there at the fountain." And the child was found at the fountain.

The wife was puzzled; she said, "How did you know?"

Freud said, "This is simple psychology. Every parent should know."

No, I cannot trust the Christian interpretation that makes God look very foolish. He must have planned it, knowing perfectly well that if Adam was prohibited from eating the fruit—if he was told, commanded, absolutely ordered to "Never touch the fruit of that tree!"—then it was absolutely certain that he would eat it.

But Adam was the first man, and was not aware of the ways of man yet. He was the first child and may have been an obedient child. There are obedient people, also. So God must have waited for a few days, and Adam did not go to the tree.

Now God must have decided to become a serpent and try through the woman, because when you cannot do anything to the man, the right way is always through the woman. He must have tried through the woman; he must have talked to Eve. And he succeeded!

That's why I say the serpent and the savior are one.

In the East, the serpent has never been in the service of the Devil; it has always been in the service of God. In the East, this is the symbology: the serpent is inside you, coiled at your sex center. It is called *kundalini*—the coiled serpent. It is there—asleep—at the lowest level, the roots. The tree of life is your spine—it holds your life; it is your trunk. It nourishes you, your energy runs through it, and the serpent is lying there at the base.

When anything stirs you it will stir the serpent, too, because that is where your energy is. So when it happens, don't be worried, don't feel guilty. Never feel guilty for anything! All that happens is good. The bad does not happen and cannot happen—the world is so full of godliness, how can the bad happen? The bad must be our interpretation.

Sex and superconsciousness are both the same energy. The serpent and the savior are not two. There is a link between the lowest and the highest. There is a sequence that leads from one to the other—a way of life,

a way of love, natural and inevitable as the way of a growing tree.

Have you watched a tree growing, how it gropes and grows upward—what method does it follow? From the seed comes the sprout, and then slowly, slowly, it starts rising upward. It comes from deep down in the earth and then it starts rising into the sky, from root to trunk and branch and leaf and flower and fruit.... This is what happens with your tree of life, too.

There is no distinction between the sacred and the profane.

There is no separation between divine love and human, four-lettered love. It is one continuity. Your love and divine love are two ends of the same phenomenon, the same energy. Your love is too muddy, true—too full of many other things like hatred, anger, jealousy, and possessiveness—true. But still it is gold—mixed with mud—but still it is gold. You have to pass through fire, and all that is not gold will be gone and only gold will remain.

Accept yourself, because only through acceptance is transformation possible. If you start feeling guilty, you will become repressive.

At the temples of Khajuraho and Konarak in India, you will see what I am talking about. These are Tantra temples, the most sacred temples that still exist on the earth. All other temples are ordinary. Only Khajuraho and Konarak, these two temples, have a message that is not ordinary, that is extraordinary—extraordinary because it is true.

What is their message?

If you have been to these temples, you will have seen illustrated on the outer sunlit walls all kinds of sexual postures—men and women

making love in so many postures, conceivable and inconceivable, possible and impossible. The walls are full of sex. You are shocked. You start thinking, "What obscenity!" You want to condemn it; you want to lower your eyes. You want to escape. But that is not because of the temple; it is because of the priests and their poisons inside you.

Go inside. As you move inside the temple, the figures become fewer and fewer, and the quality of the love starts changing. On the outer walls is pure sexuality; as you enter inside, you will find that sex is disappearing. Couples are still there—deeply in love, looking into each other's eyes, holding hands, embracing each other—but the sexuality is no longer there. Go still deeper—the figures are even fewer. Couples are there, but they are not even holding hands, not even touching. Go still deeper and the couples have disappeared. Go still deeper....

At the innermost core of the temple—what in the East is called the *gharba*, the womb—there is not a single figure. The crowd is gone; the many are gone. There is not even a window to the outside. No light comes from the outside; it is utter darkness, silence, calm, and quiet. There is not even a figure of a god—it is emptiness, it is nothingness.

The innermost core is nothingness, and the outermost circumference is a carnival. The innermost core is meditation, *samadhi*, and the outermost circumference is sexuality. This is the whole life of humanity depicted. But remember: if you destroy the outer walls, you will destroy the inner shrine, too, because the innermost silence and darkness cannot exist without the outer walls. The center of the

> *When sex is accepted naturally, it starts growing higher.*

cyclone cannot exist without the cyclone. The center cannot exist without the circumference. They are together!

Your outermost life is full of sexuality—perfectly good and perfectly beautiful! Khajuraho simply depicts you. It is the human story in stone; it is the human dance in stone—from the lowest to the highest rung of the ladder, from the many to one, from love to meditation, from the other to one's own emptiness and aloneness.

Courageous were the people who created these temples. The still point is shown together with the turning world.

The way of Tantra is neither one of blind sensuality nor only of spirituality. It is of both/and. Tantra does not support the philosophy of either/or; it supports the philosophy of both/and. It does not reject anything—it transforms everything.

Only cowards reject. If you reject something you will be that much poorer, because something will have been left untransformed. A part of you will remain ungrown; a part of you will remain childish. Your maturity will never be complete. It will be as if one leg remains on the first rung of a ladder and your hand has reached

the last rung: you will be stretched along this polarity and you will be in anguish, in agony; your life will not be of ecstasy.

That's why I preach Epicurus and Buddha together. Epicurus remains with the outer wall of the Khajuraho temple: he is right as far as he goes, but he does not go far enough. He simply takes a walk around the temple and goes home. He is not aware that he has missed the very point of the temple. Those outer walls are only outer walls; they exist to support the inner shrine.

Buddha goes into the inner shrine and sits there. In that silence he remains, but he forgets about the outer wall. And without the outer wall there is no inner shrine.

To me, both are lopsided. Something has been rejected and something has been chosen—they have not been choiceless. I say accept all—the outer and the inner, the without and the within—and you will be the richest people upon the earth.

Tantra is the way of wholeness—neither obsession with the world, nor withdrawal from it. It is being in the world lightly, with a little smile. It is playfulness. It doesn't take things seriously. It is light of heart; it laughs. It is unashamedly earthly and infinitely otherworldly. The earth and the sky meet in Tantra; it is the meeting of polar opposites.

If you go to Khajuraho, you will see it: on the face of every lover sculpted on the outer walls, there is great ecstasy. Many people go to Khajuraho and Konarak, but they only look at the lower half of these figures: they become focused on the genitalia. Few people have been able to see the whole figures. And rarely has anybody been able to see the faces of the figures, because people are so obsessed with sexuality—for or against—that they remain confined to the lower.

If you go to see Khajuraho, don't miss the faces of the lovers—they reveal the real message. Those faces are so blissful, so calm, so meditative, that you will not find such faces sculpted anywhere else. Such great ecstasy! Even the stone has bloomed in those faces; those faces have transformed the stone into rose flowers, into lotuses.

Seeing those faces you will be able to see that these lovers are no longer part of time and space; they have gone beyond.

The figures are sexually active, but they are not obsessed with sex—neither for nor against. Both are obsessions—being for or against simply mean that things are no longer natural. When things are natural, you are neither for nor against.

Are you for sleep or against sleep? If you are for, you have become unnatural; if you are against, you have become unnatural. You cannot be for or against sleep; it is a natural thing—so is sex. When sex is accepted naturally, it starts growing higher. Then one day, the bud spontaneously becomes a flower. Not that you have to *do* anything—just let the energy move, let the sap flow, and the bud will become the flower.

The Khajuraho faces are utterly at ease in a state of letting go. They are in the world, but not of it. They are not doing anything wrong; they are just like small children playing on the beach. They are playful. But sexually obsessed people have been very much against Khajuraho. Mahatma Gandhi wanted it to be covered with earth so that only once in a while, when some special guest came from another country, it could be uncovered for the guest. He thought it should be closed for ordinary people.

Now, if Mahatma Gandhi were to go to see Khajuraho, I don't think he would be able to see the faces of the figures; I don't think he would be able to go inside the temple—the outer would be enough to prevent him. I don't think he would be able to look at the outer: he would feel so angry, so guilty, so ashamed. If you talk to many of the so-called educated Indians about Khajuraho, you will find that they feel ashamed. They will say, "We are sorry, but these temples don't represent our mainstream. They are not representative of our culture. They are freak events in our culture—they don't represent us and we are sorry that they exist."

But these temples represent one of the most holistic attitudes toward life—all is accepted, because all is divine.

To me, the final stage of a human being is not the sage, not the Buddha, but Shiva Nataraj—Shiva the Dancer. Buddha has gone very deep, but the outer wall is missing, the outer wall is denied. Shiva contains all contradictions—contains the whole of existence, choicelessly. He lives in the innermost core of the shrine and he dances on the outer walls, too.

Unless the sage can dance, something is missing.

Life is a dance. You have to participate in it. The more silent you become, the deeper your participation. Never withdraw from life. Be true to life; be committed to life. Be utterly for life.

It happens when you have reached the innermost core of the temple. There is no reason for you to dance; you can remain there, silent. Just as Buddha says: When you have attained enlightenment, then two paths are open for you—either you can become an *arhat*—you can withdraw to the other shore; or you can become a *bodhisattva*—you can remain on this shore. In fact, there is no reason to be on this shore when you have become enlightened. But Buddha says, For the sake of others, for compassion's sake, create such compassion in yourself that you can linger a little longer and help people.

In the same way, when you become enlightened, two possibilities open—you can remain inside the temple, in the womb, where

it is dark and windowless. Not going out at all, not even a light penetrates; there is no sound from the outside, nothing of the marketplace. You can sit there in absolute silence, in timeless silence. There is no reason to come out and have a dance. Still, I hope that you would come back, although there is no reason. Although your journey will be complete, something will still be missing. You will have learned how to be silent—now you have to show whether you can be silent in the midst of sound. You have learned how to be alone—now you have to show whether you can be alone and love, too. You have to come back to the marketplace from the mountains. The ultimate test is there.

There is no reason for this—that I would like to repeat. There is no reason for this world, but there is a rhyme and a rhythm. No reason, but rhyme and rhythm. When you have become silent, create sound—and your silence will go deeper because of the contrasting sound. When you have known what aloneness is, be together with people—and the people and their presence will help you to know your aloneness far more deeply. When you have known how to remain still, dance—and the dance will give you the background in which the stillness will come loud and clear.

There is no reason for it, but there is a rhyme and a rhythm in it. Go to the opposite. That is the meaning of Shiva Nataraj—Shiva, the dancer of dancers. He is a buddha, but in his outer activities he is a worldly man.

This is the ultimate for Tantra, to become gods and yet be part of this world. When you can come back to the marketplace with a wine bottle in your hand, the ultimate is achieved.

HINDU AND BUDDHIST TANTRA

There are only two basic paths: the path of devotion, prayer, and love, and the path of meditation and awareness. These two different approaches persist.

Shiva's approach is that of devotion, prayer, love. Saraha's approach is that of meditation, awareness. The distinction is just a formality, because the lover and the meditator arrive at the same goal. Their arrows are released from different bows, but they reach the same target. The bow does not matter, finally. What type of bow you have chosen does not matter as long as the target is attained.

These are the two bows—the path of meditation and the path of devotion—because humans are divided into thinking and feeling. Either you can approach reality through thinking or you can approach reality through feeling.

The Buddhist approach—the approach of Buddha and Saraha—is through intelligence. It is basically through the mind that Saraha moves. Of course, the mind has to be left behind in the end, but it is the *mind* that has to be left behind. By and by, the mind has to disappear into meditation, but it is the mind that has to disappear, it is the thinking that has to be transformed and a state of no-thought has to be created. Just remember: it is a state of no-thought, and that can be created only by slowly dropping thoughts. So the whole work consists in the thinking part.

Shiva's approach is that of the feeling, of the heart. The feeling has to be transformed. Love has to be transformed so that it becomes prayerfulness. On Shiva's way, the devotee and the deity remain, but at the ultimate peak they disappear into each other. Listen to it carefully: when Shiva's Tantra reaches its ultimate orgasm, the *I* is dissolved into *Thou* and the *Thou* is dissolved into *I*—they are together, they become one unity.

When Saraha's Tantra reaches its ultimate peak, the recognition is that neither I nor Thou is right, neither I nor Thou is true, neither I nor Thou exists—both disappear. There are two zeros meeting—not *I* and *Thou* but neither *I* nor *Thou*.

Two zeros, two empty spaces, dissolve into each other because the whole effort on Saraha's path is in how to dissolve thought, and *I* and *Thou* are part of thought.

When thought is utterly dissolved, how can you call yourself *I*? And whom will you call your God? God is part of thought, God is a thought-creation, a thought-construct, a mind-construct. So all mind-constructs dissolve and *shunya*, emptiness, arises.

On Shiva's path you no longer love the form, you no longer love the person—you start loving the whole existence. The whole existence becomes your *Thou*—you are addressed to the whole existence. Possessiveness is dropped, jealousy is dropped, hatred is dropped—all that is negative in feeling is dropped. The feeling becomes purer and purer until a moment comes when there is pure love. In that moment of pure love, you dissolve into "Thou" and "Thou" dissolves into you. You also disappear, but you disappear not like two zeros, you disappear as

the beloved disappears into the lover and the lover disappears into the beloved.

Up to this point the paths are different, but that too is just a formal difference. Beyond this, what does it matter whether you disappear like a lover and a beloved or you disappear like two zeros? The basic point, the fundamental point, is that you disappear, nothing is left, no trace is left. That disappearance is enlightenment.

So you have to understand this: if love appeals to you, Shiva will appeal to you and *The Book of Secrets* will be your Tantra bible. If meditation appeals to you, then Saraha will appeal to you. Both are right, both are going on the same journey. With whom you would like to travel—that is your choice.

If you can be alone and blissful, then choose Saraha; if you cannot be blissful when you are alone, if your bliss comes only when you relate, then choose Shiva.

This is the difference between Hindu Tantra and Buddhist Tantra.

saraha, founder of buddhist tantra

You may not have heard the name of Saraha, but Saraha is the founder of Tantra. He is one of the great benefactors of humanity. Born about two centuries after Buddha, he was a branch of the great tree that started with Gautam Buddha. One branch moves from Buddha to Mahakashyap to Bodhidharma, where Zen was born—and it is still full of flowers, that branch. Another branch moves from Buddha to his son, Rahul Bhadra, from Rahul Bhadra to Sri Kirti, and from Sri Kirti to Saraha. From Saraha it moved to Nargarjuna and Tilopa—that is the Tantra branch of the tree planted by Buddha. It is still bearing fruit in Tibet. Tantra converted Tibet and Saraha is the founder of Tantra just as Bodhidharma is the founder of Zen. Bodhidharma conquered China, Korea, Japan. Saraha conquered Tibet.

A few things about Saraha's life: He was born in Vidarbha, which is part of Maharashtra state in India near Pune. When King Mahapala was the ruler of Maharashtra, Saraha was born to a very learned Brahmin who was in the king's court. The father was in the court, so the young man grew up there; he had four other brothers and they were all great scholars. Saraha was the youngest child and the most intelligent of them all. The four older brothers were nothing compared with Saraha. The four matured and got married. Saraha's fame was spreading all over the country and the king was enchanted by him. He was willing to give his own daughter in marriage to Saraha, but Saraha wanted to renounce everything to become a *sannyasin*, a wandering seeker.

The king was hurt; he tried to persuade Saraha to remain. This young man was so beautiful and so intelligent, it was because of him that Mahapala's court was becoming famous. The king was worried; he didn't want this young man to become a sannyasin. He wanted to protect him and give him all the comforts possible —he was ready to do anything for him. But Saraha persisted, and permission had to be given —he became a sannyasin and a disciple of Sri Kirti.

Sri Kirti is in the direct lineage of Buddha— first Gautam Buddha, then his son Rahul Bhadra, and then Sri Kirti. There were just two masters between Saraha and Buddha, so the tree must have been very green; the vibration must have been very much alive. Buddha had just recently left; the climate must have been full of his fragrance.

The king was shocked, because Saraha was a Brahmin—if he wanted to become a sannyasin he should have become a Hindu sannyasin, but instead he chose a Buddhist master, Sri Kirti. The first thing Sri Kirti told Saraha was, "Forget all your Vedas, all your learning, all that nonsense." It was difficult for Saraha, but he was ready to stake everything. Something about the presence of Sri Kirti had attracted him like a great magnet. He dropped all his learning; he became unlearned again.

This is one of the greatest renunciations—it is easy to renounce wealth, it is easy to renounce a great kingdom, but to renounce knowledge is the most difficult thing in the world. In the first place, how can you renounce it? It is there inside you. You can escape from your kingdom, you can go to the Himalayas, you can distribute your wealth—but how can you renounce your knowledge? It is so painful to become ignorant again. It is the greatest austerity there is, to become ignorant again, to become again innocent like a child. But Saraha was ready.

Years passed, and by and by he erased all that he had known. He became a great meditator. Just as he had started to become famous as a great scholar, now his fame as a great meditator started spreading. People started coming from far and away just to have

a glimpse of this young man who had become so innocent, like a fresh leaf, like dewdrops on the grass in the morning.

One day while Saraha was meditating, he saw a vision—a vision of a woman in the marketplace who was going to be his real teacher. Sri Kirti had just put him on the path, but the real teaching was to come from a woman.

Now, this has to be understood. Only Tantra has never been male chauvinistic. In fact, to go into Tantra you need the cooperation of a wise woman; without a wise woman, you will not be able to enter the complex world of Tantra.

Saraha had a vision that his teacher would be a woman in the marketplace. First, a woman and second, in the marketplace! Tantra thrives in the marketplace, in the thick of life. It is not an attitude of negation; it is utter positivity.

Saraha stood up to leave. Sri Kirti asked him, "Where are you going?"

Saraha said, "You have shown me the path—you took my learning away. You have done half the work—you have cleaned my slate. Now I am ready for the other half." With the blessings of Sri Kirti, who was laughing, Saraha went away. He went to the marketplace and he was surprised: he really found the woman that

he had seen in the vision! The woman was making an arrow; she was an arrowsmith.

The third thing to be remembered about Tantra is that the more cultured, the more civilized a person, the less likely that person's Tantric transformation. The less civilized, the more primitive, the more alive a person is. The more you become civilized, the more you become plastic—you become artificial. If you become too cultivated, you lose your roots in the earth. You are afraid of the muddy world and you start posing as though you are not of the world. Tantra says that in order to find the real person, you will have to go to the roots. Those who are still uncivilized, uneducated, uncultured are more alive; they have more vitality. In the world of those who are still primitive, there is a possibility of starting to grow. You have grown in a wrong direction and they have not grown yet—they can still choose the right direction, therefore they have more potential. They don't have anything to undo; they can proceed directly.

An arrowsmith woman in India is a low-caste woman, and for Saraha—a learned Brahmin, a famous Brahmin, who had belonged to the court of a king—going to an arrowsmith woman was symbolic. The learned has to go to the vital. The plastic has to go to the real.

He saw this woman—a young woman, very alive, radiant with life—cutting an arrow shaft, looking neither to the right nor to the left, but wholly absorbed in making the arrow. He immediately felt something extraordinary in her presence, something that he had never come across. Even his master Sri Kirti paled before the presence of this woman. Something so fresh, something from the very source....

Sri Kirti was a great philosopher. Yes, he had told Saraha to drop all his learning, but still he was a learned man. He had told Saraha to drop all the Vedas and scriptures, but he had his own

> *Those who are still uncivilized, uncultured, are more alive; they have more vitality.*

scriptures and his own Vedas. Even though he was anti-philosophical, his anti-philosophy was a sort of philosophy. Now, here was a woman who was neither philosophical nor anti-philosophical —who simply did not know what philosophy

was, who was blissfully unaware of the world of philosophy, of the world of thought. She was a woman of action and she was utterly absorbed in her action.

Saraha watched carefully: The arrow ready, the woman closed one eye and opened the other, assumed the posture of aiming at an invisible target. Saraha came still closer. Now, there was no target; she was simply posing. She had closed one eye, her other eye was open, and she was aiming at some unknown, invisible target.

Saraha started sensing some message. This posture was symbolic, he felt, but the meaning of it was very dim and dark. He could feel something there, but he could not figure out what it was.

He asked the woman whether she was a professional arrowsmith, and the woman laughed, a wild laugh, and said, "You stupid Brahmin! You have left the Vedas, but now you are worshipping Buddha's sayings. So what is the point? You have changed your books, you have changed your philosophy, but you remain the same stupid man."

Saraha was shocked. Nobody had ever talked to him that way. Only an uncultured woman can talk that way. And the way she laughed was so uncivilized, so primitive—but still, very much alive. He was feeling pulled. She was a great magnet and he was a piece of iron. Then she said, "You think you are a Buddhist?" He must have been wearing the robe of the Buddhist monk, a yellow robe. She laughed again. She said, "Buddha's meaning can only be known through action, not through words and not through books. Are you not yet at the point where enough is enough? Are you not yet fed up with all this? Don't waste any more time in that futile search. Come and follow me!"

Then something happened, something like a communion. Saraha had never felt like that before. In that moment, the spiritual significance of what she was doing dawned on him. Neither looking to the left, nor looking to the right, he had seen her—just looking in the middle. For the first time he understood what Buddha meant by being in the middle, avoiding the extremes. First he had been a philosopher, then he had become an anti-philosopher—from one extreme to another. First he was worshipping one thing, now he was worshipping just the opposite, but the worship continued.

You can move from the left to the right, from the right to the left, but that is not going to help. You will be like a pendulum moving from left to right, from right to left... and have you observed? When the pendulum is going to the right, it is gaining momentum to go to the left; when it is going to the left it is again gaining momentum to go to the right. And the clock continues, the world continues.

To be in the middle means the pendulum just hangs there in the middle, moving neither to the right nor to the left. Then the clock stops. Then the world stops. Then there is no more time; then the state of no-time arises. Saraha

had heard it said so many times by Sri Kirti; he had read about it, he had pondered it, contemplated it. He had argued with others about it, that to be in the middle is the right thing. For the first time he had seen it in action. The woman was not looking to the right and not looking to the left... she was just looking in the middle, focused in the middle.

The middle is the point from which transcendence happens. Think about it, contemplate it, watch it in life. A person is running after money, mad, money-mad; money is the only god. One day or other, the god fails—it is bound to fail. Money cannot be your god; it is an illusion, you are projecting. One day you realize that there is no god in money—there is nothing in it and you have been wasting your life. Then you turn against it, you take the opposite attitude, you won't touch money. Both ways you are obsessed. Now you are *against* money, but the obsession remains. You have moved from the left to the right, but money is still at the center of your consciousness.

You can change from one desire to another. You were too worldly, now you become otherworldly—but *you* remain the same, the disease persists.

Buddha says, To be worldly is to be worldly, and to be otherworldly is also to be worldly; to worship money is to be mad, to be against money is to be mad; to seek power is foolish, to escape from it is also foolish.

Just to be in the middle is what wisdom is all about. For the first time Saraha actually saw it— he had not even seen it in Sri Kirti. And the woman was right. She said, "You can only learn through action." She was so utterly absorbed

that she was not even looking at Saraha, who was standing there watching her. She was utterly absorbed; she was totally in the action.

That is again a Buddhist message: To be total in action is to be free of action. Karma is created because you are not totally in your acts. If you are totally in an action, it leaves no trace.

Do anything totally and not only is it finished, but also you will not carry the psychological memory of it. Do anything incompletely and it stays with you, it goes on and becomes a hangover. The mind wants to continue and complete it. Mind has a great temptation to complete things. Complete anything, and the mind is gone. If you continue doing things totally, one day you suddenly find there is no mind. Mind is the accumulated past of all incomplete actions. You wanted to love a

woman and you didn't love; now the woman is gone. You wanted to go to your father and to be forgiven for all that you had done in such a way that he was hurt; now he is dead.

The hangover will remain with you like a ghost. Now you are helpless—what to do? Whom to go to, and how to ask forgiveness? You wanted to be kind to a friend but you could not because you became closed. Now the friend is no more, and it hurts. You start to feel guilty. You repent. Things go on like this.

Do any action totally and you are free of it; you don't look back because there is nothing to see. You have no hangovers. You simply go ahead. Your eyes are clear of the past; your vision is not clouded. In that clarity, you will come to know what reality is.

You are so worried... with all your incomplete actions you are like a junkyard. One thing is incomplete here, another thing is incomplete there—nothing is complete.

Have you observed it? Have you ever completed anything, or is everything incomplete? We push aside one thing and start something else, and before this is complete we start another. We become more and more burdened—this is what karma is. Karma means incomplete action.

Be total and you will be free.

The arrowsmith woman was totally absorbed. That's why she looked so luminous— she was so beautiful. She was an ordinary woman but her beauty was not of this earth. Her beauty was because of her total absorption in her action. The beauty was because she was not an extremist. The beauty was because she was in the middle, balanced. Out of balance comes grace.

> *Do any action totally and you are free of it. You don't look back because there is nothing to see.*

For the first time, Saraha had encountered a woman who was not just physically beautiful, but who was spiritually beautiful—absorbed totally, absorbed in whatever she was doing. He understood for the first time: This is what meditation is! Not that you sit for a special period of time and repeat a mantra, not that you go to the church or to the temple or to

years, psychology has come to the same understanding that Buddha had so long ago—Buddha says that half the brain reasons and half the brain intuits. The brain is divided in two parts, two hemispheres. The left side holds the faculty of reason, logic, discursive thought, analysis, philosophy, theology... words and words and words, and arguments

the mosque—but to be in life, to go on doing trivial things, but with such absorption that the profundity is revealed in every action. He understood meditation for the first time. He had been meditating, he had been struggling hard, but for the first time meditation was there in front of him, alive. He could feel it; he could have touched it. It was almost tangible.

Closing one eye and opening the other is a Buddhist symbol. Buddha says—and psychologists agree with him now; after 2500

and syllogisms and inferences. The left side of the brain is Aristotelian. The right side is intuitive, poetic—from there comes inspiration, vision, a priori consciousness, a priori awareness. Not that you argue—you simply come to *know*. Not that you infer—you simply *realize*. That is the meaning of a priori awareness; it is simply *there*. The truth is *known* by the right side of the brain; truth is *inferred* by the left side. Inference is just inference, it is not experience.

Suddenly Saraha realized that the woman had closed one eye as a symbol of closing the eye of reason, logic. And she had opened the other eye, symbolic of love, intuition, awareness.

Then he realized something about her posture. Aiming at the unknown, at the invisible, we are on the journey toward knowing the unknown—toward knowing that which cannot

be known. That is real knowledge—to know that which cannot be known, to realize that which is unrealizable, to attain that which cannot be attained. This impossible passion is what makes a person a spiritual seeker.

Yes, it is impossible. By "impossible," I don't mean that it will not happen; I mean that it cannot happen unless you are utterly transformed. As you are, it cannot happen, but there are different ways of being, and you can be totally new. Then it happens. It is possible

for a different kind of human being. That's why Jesus said that until you are reborn, you will not know it. A new human being will know it.

As you are, you will have to disappear. Then the new is born, a new consciousness comes in because there is something indestructible in you; nobody can destroy it. Only the destructible will be destroyed and the indestructible will be there. When you attain to that indestructible element in your being, to that eternal awareness in your being, you are a new consciousness. Through that consciousness the impossible is possible, the unattainable is attained.

So Saraha noted the woman's posture. Aiming at the unknown, the invisible, the unknowable, the one—that is the target. How to be one with existence? The nondual is the target, where subject and object are lost, where "I and Thou" are lost.

There is a great book by Martin Buber entitled *I And Thou*. Martin Buber says the experience of prayer is an *I–Thou* experience— he is right. God is the *Thou* and you remain an *I*. You have a dialogue, a communion with the *Thou*. But Buddhism has no prayer in it. Buddhism goes higher than prayer. It says: Even when there is an *I–Thou* relationship, you remain divided, you remain separate. You can shout at each other, but there will be no communion. The communion happens only when the *I–Thou* division is no more; when subject and object disappear; where there is no *I* and no *Thou*, no seeker and no sought... when there is unity, unison.

Saraha said to her, "You are not an ordinary arrowsmith woman. I am sorry to have even

thought that you were an ordinary arrowsmith woman. Excuse me, I am tremendously sorry. You are a great master and I am reborn through you. Till yesterday I was not a real Brahmin; from today I am. You are my master and you are my mother and you have given me a new birth. I am no longer the same."

The arrowsmith woman accepted him. She had been waiting for Saraha to come. They moved to a cremation ground and started living together.

Why to a cremation ground? Because unless you understand death you will not be able to understand life. Unless you die, you will not be reborn. After Saraha, many Tantra disciples have lived on the cremation ground because he was the founder, and he lived on a cremation ground. Dead bodies would be brought and burned, yet he lived there; that was his home. He lived with the arrowsmith woman; they lived together. There was great love between them— not the love of a woman and a man, but the love of a master and a disciple, which is certainly higher than any man-woman love can ever reach. Which is more intimate—certainly more intimate—because a man-woman love affair is between bodies; at the most, sometimes it encompasses the mind; otherwise, it remains in the body. But disciple and a master—it is a love affair of souls. Saraha had found his soulmate. They were in tremendous love, great love, which rarely happens on the earth. She taught him Tantra.

Only a woman can truly teach Tantra. Sometimes a man can become a Tantra teacher, but he will have to become very feminine. A woman is already feminine; she already has those loving, affectionate qualities; she naturally has that care, that love, that feeling for the soft. Saraha became a tantrika under the guidance of the arrowsmith woman. He was no longer meditating. One day he had left behind all the Vedas, scriptures, and knowledge; now he left behind even meditation. Rumors started spreading all over the country: "He no longer meditates. He sings, of course, and dances, too, but no meditation anymore." Now singing was his meditation. Now dancing was his meditation. Now celebration was his whole lifestyle.

Living in a cremation ground and celebrating? Living where only death happens and living joyously? This is the beauty of Tantra—it joins together the opposites, the contraries, the contradictories. If you go to the cremation ground you will feel sad; it will be difficult for you to be joyous. It will be difficult for you to sing and dance where people are being cremated and their friends and relatives are crying and weeping. Every day death and more death, all day and night, death. How can you rejoice?

But if you cannot rejoice there, then all that you think is your joy is just make-believe. If you can rejoice there, then joy has *really* happened to you. Now it is unconditional. Now it doesn't make any difference whether death happens or life, whether somebody is born or somebody is dying.

Saraha started singing and dancing. He was no longer serious—Tantra is not serious. Tantra is playfulness. Yes, it is sincere—but not serious. It is joyous. Play entered Saraha's being. Tantra is play, because Tantra is a highly evolved form of love. Love is play.

There are people who would not like even love to be playful. Many religions say you should make love only when you want to reproduce. Even love they change into work—"reproduction." This is just ugly! Make love only when you want to reproduce—is the woman a factory!? *Reproduction*—the very word is ugly. Love is fun! Make love when you are feeling happy, joyous, when you are at the top of the world. Share that energy. Love your partner when you have that quality of dance and song and joy—not for reproduction! The word *reproduction* is obscene! Make love out of joy, out of abundant joy. Give when you have it.

Play entered into Saraha's being. A lover always has a spirit of play. The moment the spirit of play dies, you become a husband or a wife.

RAHUL BECOMES SARAHA

Saraha's original name was Rahul, the name given by his father. The arrowsmith woman called him Saraha. *Saraha* is a beautiful word. It means "he who has shot the arrow." The moment he recognized the significance of the woman's actions, those symbolic gestures, the moment he could read and decode what the woman was trying to give him, what the woman was trying to show him, the woman was tremendously happy. She danced and said, "Now, from today, you will be called Saraha: you have shot the arrow. Understanding the significance of my actions, you have penetrated the truth."

> *Tantra is play, because Tantra is a highly evolved form of love. Love is play.*

Then you are no longer lovers; then you reproduce. The moment you become a husband or a wife, something beautiful has gone dead. It is no longer alive, the juice flows no more. Now it is pretension, hypocrisy.

Play entered Saraha's being, and through play, true religion was born. His ecstasy was so infectious that people started coming to watch him dancing and singing. When people came to watch, they would also start dancing and singing with him. The cremation ground became a place of great celebration. Yes, bodies were still being burned, but more and more people started gathering around Saraha and the arrowsmith woman, and great joy was created.

It became so infectious that people who had never heard anything about ecstasy would come, dance and sing, and fall into ecstasy. His very vibration, his very presence, became so potent that if you were ready to participate with him, it would happen… it was a contact high. He was so drunk that his inner drunkenness started overflowing to other people. He was so stoned that others started becoming more and more stoned.

Then the inevitable happened: the Brahmins and the priests and the scholars and the righteous people started vilifying and slandering him. I say inevitable because whenever there is a man like Saraha, the scholars are going to be against him, the priests are going to be against him, and the so-called moral people—puritans, self-righteous people—will be against him. They started spreading absolutely baseless rumors about him. They started saying to people, "He has fallen from grace. He is a pervert. He is no longer a Brahmin. He has given up celibacy. He is no longer even a Buddhist monk. He indulges in shameful practices with a low-caste woman and runs around like a mad dog in all directions." His ecstasy looked like a mad dog to them—it all depends on how you interpret things. He was dancing all over the cremation ground. He was mad, but he was not a mad dog—he was a mad god! It depends on how you see it.

The king was anxious to know exactly what was happening. More and more people had been coming to him. They knew that the king had always been deeply respectful toward Saraha and that he had wanted to appoint him as his counselor in the court, but that Saraha had renounced the world. The king was worried. He loved the young man and respected him, and he was concerned. So he sent a few people to persuade Saraha: "Come back to your old ways. You are a Brahmin, your father was a great scholar, and you yourself were a great scholar—what are you doing? You have gone astray. Come back home. The king wants you to go back to the palace and be part of his family. What you are doing is not good."

It is said that Saraha sang one hundred sixty verses to those people who had come to convert him. Upon hearing those one hundred sixty verses, the people started dancing and they never went home! Now the king was even more worried.

The queen had also always been interested in the young man. She wanted him to marry her daughter, so she went to see him. Saraha sang eighty verses to the queen and she never went home. Now the king was *really* puzzled: "What is going on?" Finally the king himself went to the cremation ground, and Saraha sang forty verses for him. And the king started dancing on the cremation ground like a mad dog.

So there are three scriptures in the name of Saraha: first, *The People's Song of Saraha*, one hundred sixty verses. Second, *The Queen's Song of Saraha*, eighty verses; and finally, *The Royal Song of Saraha*. There were one hundred sixty verses for the people because their understanding was not great; eighty for the queen—she was a little higher, her understanding was a deeper; and forty verses for the king because he was a man of intelligence, awareness, and understanding.

Because the king was converted, the whole country, by and by, was converted. And it is said in the old scriptures that a time came when the whole country became empty. Empty?!—it is a Buddhist word. It means people became nobodies, they lost their ego-trips. People started enjoying the moment. The hustle and bustle, the competitive violence, disappeared from the country. It became a silent country. It became empty... as if no one were there. The "people" as such disappeared; a great godliness descended on the country. These verses of Saraha were at the root of it, the very source of it.

saraha's royal song

Listen to this beautiful verse from Saraha:

Though the house lamps have been lit,
the blind live on in the dark.
Though spontaneity is all-encompassing and close,
To the deluded it remains always far away.

He says: Look! I have become enlightened. Though the house lamps have been lit... my innermost core is no longer dark. See! There is great light in me; my soul is awakened. I am no more the same Rahul you used to know. I am Saraha; my arrow has reached the target.

Though the house lamps have been lit,
the blind live on in the dark.

But what can I do? Saraha says. If somebody is blind, even when the house lamps are lit he goes on living in darkness. The lamps are not missing, but his eyes are closed. So don't listen to blind people—just open your eyes and look at me. See the person standing in front of you, whom you are confronting. The blind live on in the dark, though the house lamps have been lit.

Though spontaneity is all-encompassing and close...

And I am so close to you... the spontaneity is so close to you, you can already touch it and eat it and drink it. You can dance with me and you can move into ecstasy with me. I am so close— you may not find spontaneity so close again!

... to the deluded it remains always far away.

They talk about enlightenment and they read the Patanjali Sutras; they talk about great things, but whenever a great thing happens they are against it.

This is something strange about humans. Humans are strange animals. You can appreciate Buddha, but if Buddha comes and confronts you, you will not be able to appreciate him at all—you may go against him, you may become his enemy. Why?

When you read a book about Buddha, everything is okay—the book is in your hands. When a living buddha has to be confronted, he is not in your hands—you are falling into his hands. Hence the fear, resistance, and desire to escape. The best way to escape is to convince yourself that he has gone wrong, something is wrong with him. That is the only way to escape—if you can prove to yourself that he is wrong. You can find a thousand and one

things in a buddha that look wrong because you are squinting and you are blind and your mind is in turmoil. You can project anything.

Now this man has attained buddhahood, and everybody is talking about the low-caste woman. They have not looked into that woman's reality. They have only been thinking about the fact that she is an arrowsmith woman, low-caste, a *sudra*, untouchable. How can a Brahmin touch an untouchable woman? How can the Brahmin live there? They have heard that the woman cooks food for him—this is a great sin, this is a great fall, a Brahmin eating food cooked by a sudra, an untouchable, a low-caste woman!

And why should a Brahmin live on the cremation ground? Brahmins live in the temples and in the palaces as part of the court. Why on the cremation ground?—a dirty place, with skulls and dead bodies all around. This is perversion!

But they have not looked into the fact that unless you understand death you will never be able to understand life.

When you have looked deeply into death and found that life is never dead, when you have penetrated deeply into death and found that life continues even after death,

> ❝ Don't listen to blind people—
> just open your eyes and look. ❞

that death makes no difference, that death is immaterial....

People don't know anything about life—life is eternal, timeless. Only the body dies, so only the dead dies; the alive continues. For this understanding, you have to go into a deep experimentation—but these people would not look at that. They heard that Saraha was participating in strange practices. They must have gossiped and exaggerated; things must have gotten out of hand, and everyone must have been multiplying the gossip.

And there are plenty of Tantra practices that can be gossiped about! In Tantra, the man sits in front of the naked woman and he has to watch her so deeply, to see her through and through, that all desire to look at a woman naked disappears.

Then the man is free from the form. This is a great secret technique; otherwise, you go on continuously seeing the woman naked in your mind. Each woman that passes by on the road, you want to undress her—that idea will be there.

Now suddenly you see Saraha sitting before a naked woman—how will you interpret it? You will interpret it according to yourself. You will say, "So okay, he is doing what we always wanted to do but didn't, so we are better than him. At least we are not doing it. Of course we fantasize sometimes, but it is only in thought, not in deed. He has fallen." You will not miss the opportunity to gossip about it.

But what is Saraha really doing? It is a secret science. By watching, for months together, the tantrika will meditate on the woman's body, her form, he will meditate on her beauty. He will

look at everything, whatever he wants to look at. Do the breasts have some appeal? He will look and meditate on the breasts. He has to get rid of the form and the only way to get rid of the form is to know it so deeply that it has no attraction anymore.

Now something just the opposite is happening from what the gossipers are saying. Saraha is going beyond.

Never again will he want to undress a woman, not even in his mind, not even in a dream. That obsession will not be there. But the crowd, the mob, has its own ideas. Ignorant, unaware, they go on talking about things they don't understand.

Though spontaneity is all-encompassing and close,
To the deluded it remains always far away.
Though there may be many rivers, they are one in the sea,
Though there may be many lies, one truth will conquer all.
When one sun appears, the dark,
However deep, will vanish.

Saraha says: Just look at me—the sun has risen. So I know, howsoever deep your darkness, it is going to vanish also. Look at me—the truth is born in me! You may have heard thousands of lies about me, but one truth will conquer them all.

Though there may be many rivers, they are one in the sea.

Just come close to me. Let your river drop into my ocean, and you will have my taste.

Though there may be many lies, one truth will conquer all.

Truth is one, only lies are many. Only lies can be many. Truth cannot be many. Health is one; diseases are many. One health conquers all diseases and one truth conquers all lies.

When one sun appears, the dark,
However deep, will vanish.

In these four verses, Saraha has invited the king to enter into his inner being; he has opened his heart. And he says: I am not here to convince you logically, I am here to convince you existentially. I will not give any proof and I will not say anything in defense of myself. The heart is open—you come in and see what has happened. So close is spontaneity, so close is God, so close is truth. The sun has risen—open your eyes!

Remember, a mystic has no proof.

He cannot have any proof by the very nature of things. He is the only proof… so all he can do is to bare his heart to you.

These verses, these songs of Saraha, have to be meditated on deeply. Each song can become

the opening of a flower in your heart. The king was liberated—so can you be. Saraha has penetrated the target. You can also penetrate the target. You can also become a Saraha—one whose arrow has been shot.

As a cloud that rises from the sea
Absorbing rain, the earth embraces,
So, like the sky, the sea remains
Without increasing or decreasing.

He is saying to the king: Look at the sky. There are two phenomena, the sky and the cloud. The cloud comes and goes. The sky never comes and never goes. The cloud is there sometimes, and sometimes it is not there; it is a time phenomenon, it is momentary. The sky is always there; it is a timeless phenomenon, it is eternity. The clouds cannot corrupt it, not even the black clouds can corrupt it. There is no possibility of corrupting it; its purity is absolute, its purity is untouchable. Its purity is always virgin; you cannot violate it. Clouds can come and go, and they have been coming and going, but the sky is as pure as ever; not even a trace is left behind.

So there are two things in existence: one is like the sky, and one is like the cloud. Your actions are like the cloud—they come and go. You? You are like the sky: you never come and you never go. Your birth and your death are like the clouds, they *happen*. You? You never happen; you are *always* there. Things happen *in* you, *you* never happen.

Things happen just like clouds happen in the sky. You are the silent watcher of the play of clouds. Sometimes they are white and beautiful and sometimes they are dark and dismal and ugly. Sometimes they are full of rain and

> *You are focused on the cloud but you have forgotten the sky.*

sometimes they are empty. Sometimes they greatly benefit the earth and sometimes they cause great harm. Sometimes they bring floods and destruction and sometimes they bring life, greenery, crops. But the sky remains always the same: good or bad, divine or devilish, the clouds don't corrupt the sky.

Actions are clouds. Doings are clouds.
Being is like the sky.

Saraha is saying: Look at my sky! Don't look at my actions. It needs a shift of awareness, nothing else—just a shift of awareness. It needs a change of gestalt. You are looking at the cloud, you are focused on the cloud, but you have forgotten the sky. Then suddenly you remember the sky—you drop your focus on the cloud and you focus on the sky. Then the cloud becomes irrelevant; then you are in a totally different dimension.

Just a shift of focus... and the world is different. When you watch a person's behavior, you are focusing on the cloud. When you watch the innermost purity of the person's being, you are watching the sky. If you watch the innermost purity, then you will never see anyone evil, then the whole of existence is holy. If you see the actions, then you cannot see anyone holy. Even the holiest person is prone to commit many errors as far as actions are concerned. If you watch the actions, you can find wrong actions in Jesus, in Buddha, in Mahavira, in Krishna, in Rama. Then even the greatest saint will look like a sinner.

There are many books written about Jesus; he is the object of thousands of studies. Many are written to prove he is the only begotten son of God—and of course they can prove it. Then many are written to prove that he is just a neurotic and nothing else—they can also prove it. And all are talking about the same person! What is happening? How do they manage? One party chooses the white clouds, another party chooses the black clouds—and both are there, because no action can be just white or just black. To be, it has to be both.

Whatever you do will bring some good into the world and will bring some bad into the world—whatever you do. Just in making the choice to do something, many things will be good and many things will be wrong after that choice is made. Think of any action: you give some money to a beggar—you are doing good. But the beggar then purchases some poison and commits suicide. Your intention was good, but the total result is bad. You help a man who is ill by taking him to the hospital. Then when he is healthy, he commits murder. Now, without your help there would have been one murder less in the world. Your intention was good, but the total result is bad.

So do we judge by the intention or do we judge by the result? And who knows about your intention? Intention is internal... maybe deep down you were hoping that when this man got healthy he would commit a murder.

Sometimes it happens that your intention is bad and the result is good. You threw a rock at a person who had been suffering from migraine for many years, and the rock hit his head. Since then, his migraine has disappeared. Now what to do? What to say about your act? Was it moral? Immoral? You wanted to kill the man, but you could only kill the migraine.

That's how acupuncture was born. A great science, one of the most beneficial boons to humanity, was born in this way. A man had been suffering from headaches for many years. And another man, his enemy, wanted to kill him. Hiding behind a tree, the enemy shot an arrow; the arrow hit the man's leg and he fell down... but his headache disappeared. The people who were looking after him and the doctors of the town were puzzled as to how it happened. By chance, by coincidence, the arrow had hit an acupuncture point on the leg and the inner electrical flow of the man's body energy changed. Because the inner flow of the electricity changed, his headache disappeared.

That's why when you go to the acupuncturist and say, "I have a headache," she may not touch your head at all. She may start pressing your feet or your hand, or she may needle your hand or your back. And you will be surprised: "What are you doing? My head is the trouble, not my back!" But she knows better. The whole body is an interconnected electrical phenomenon; there are hundreds of points, and she knows where to stimulate the energy to change the flow. Everything is interconnected.

But this is how acupuncture was born. The man who shot the arrow at his enemy—was he a great saint or was he a sinner? Difficult to say. If you look at actions, it is up to you. You can choose the good ones or you can choose the bad ones. In the overall reality, each act brings something good and something bad.

In fact, this is my understanding—meditate on it—whatever you do, the goodness of it and the badness of it are always in the same proportion. Let me repeat: good and bad are always in the same proportion, because they are two aspects of the same coin. You may do

good—but something bad is bound to happen, because where will the other aspect go? You may do bad—but some good is bound to happen, because where will the other aspect go? The coin exists with both aspects together; a single aspect cannot exist alone.

Sinners are sometimes beneficial and saints are sometimes harmful. Saints and sinners are both in the same boat! Once you understand this, a change is possible. Then you won't look at the actions. If the proportion is the same whether you do good or bad, then what is the point of judging a man by his actions? Change the whole emphasis and move to another gestalt—the sky.

That's what Saraha is saying to the king. He is saying: Right you are! People have told you these things and they are not wrong. I run around like a mad dog! Yes, if you just watch the action you will be misguided; you will not be able to understand me. Watch my inner sky. Watch my inner priority. Watch my inner core. That's the only way to see the truth. Yes, I live with this woman, and ordinarily living with a woman means what it means. But this is no ordinary living together. There is no man-woman relationship at all; it has nothing to do with sexuality. We live together as two spaces, we live together as two freedoms; we live together as two empty boats. But you have to look into the sky, not into the clouds.

As a cloud that rises from the sea
absorbing rain, the earth embraces.
So, like the sky, the sea remains
without increasing or decreasing.

And another thing Saraha reminds him of: Watch the sea. Millions of clouds rise out of the sea, so much water evaporates, but the sea does not decrease because of that. The clouds will rain on the earth, rivulets will become great rivers, many rivers will be flooded, and the water will rush back to the ocean, to the sea. All the rivers of the earth will pour their water into the sea, but that does not make the sea increase—the sea remains the same. Whether something is taken out of it or something is poured into it makes no difference; its perfection is such that you cannot take anything out of it and you cannot add anything to it.

Saraha is saying: Look! The inner being is so perfect that your actions may be those of a sinner, but nothing is taken away. Your actions may be those of a saint, but nothing is added to you. You remain the same.

It is a tremendously revolutionary saying. It is a great statement. Saraha says: Nothing can be added to you and nothing can be deleted from you, your inner perfection is such. You cannot become more beautiful and you cannot become ugly. You cannot become rich and you cannot become poor. You are like the sea.

One of the Buddhist sutras, Vaipulya Sutra, describes two very costly jewels in the ocean: one jewel prevents the ocean from becoming less when water is drawn from it, and the other keeps it from becoming too large when water flows into it. Those two great jewels prevent these things from happening: the ocean never becomes less and it never becomes more. It is so vast, it does not matter how many clouds arise out of it and how much water evaporates. It is so vast, it does not matter how many rivers fall into it and bring great amounts of water. It remains the same.

Such is the inner core of your being. Such is the inner core of existence. Increase and decrease are on the periphery, not at the center. You can accumulate great knowledge or you can remain ignorant; that is only on the periphery. No knowledge can make you more knowing than you already are. Nothing can be added to you. Your purity is infinite; there is no way to improve upon it.

This is the Tantra vision. This is the core of the Tantra attitude: you are as you are; there is no hankering for improvement. Not that you have to become good, not that you have to change this and that—you have to accept all, and remember your sky, remember your sea. By and by, an understanding arises, when you know what is a cloud and what is the sky, what is a river and what is the sea. Once you are in tune with your sea, all anxiety disappears, all guilt disappears. You become innocent like a child.

The king had known Saraha as a great man of knowledge, and now he was behaving like an ignorant man. He had stopped reciting his Vedas, he no longer did the rituals that his religion prescribed, he no longer even meditated. He was doing nothing that was ordinarily thought to be religious. What was he doing here, living on a cremation ground, dancing and singing like a madman, and doing so many untraditional things? Where had his knowledge gone?

Saraha says: You can take all my knowledge away and it will not make any difference because I am not lessened by it. Or you can bring all the scriptures of the world and pour them into me and that won't make any difference. I won't become more because of that.

> *The mask has to be put aside.*
> *Hence, a love and a trust is needed—*
> *that you can be utterly nude, without*
> *any fear.*

He had been a respectable man, the whole kingdom had respected him; and suddenly he had become one of the most disreputable men. Yet Saraha says: You can give me all the honors that are possible, and nothing is added to me. Or you can take all the honors away and insult me. You can do whatever you want to destroy my respectability, but nothing is happening to me. No matter what, I remain the same. I am that which never increases and never decreases. Now I know that I am not the cloud,

I am the sky. I am not much worried whether people think the cloud is black or white, because I am not the cloud. I am not the small river, the tiny river, or a tiny pool of water… I am not a cup of tea.

Storms arise in a cup of tea very easily, it is so tiny. Take just one spoonful out of it and something is lost; pour in one more spoonful and it is too much and spills out. Saraha says: I am the vast sea. Take whatever you want to take, or give whatever you want to give—either way it does not matter.

Look at the beauty of it! The moment nothing matters, you have come home. If something still matters, you are far away from home. If you are still watching and being cunning and clever about your actions—you have to do this and you have not to do that, and there are still shoulds and should-nots—then you are far away from home. You still think of yourself in terms of the momentary and not in terms of the eternal.

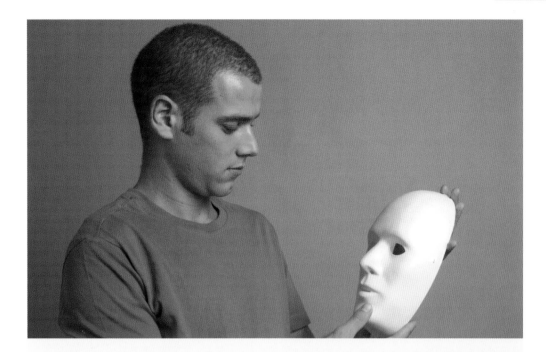

BEING AND ACTION

Tantra believes in being, not in action and character, because once being is transformed, actions are transformed. That is the only way to change your actions. Who has ever been able to change his actions directly? You can only pretend.

If you have anger in you and you want to change your action, what will you do? You will suppress the anger and you will show a false face; you will have to wear a mask. If you have sexuality in you, what will you do to change it? You can take a vow of celibacy and you can pretend, but deep down the volcano continues. You are sitting on a volcano that can erupt any moment. You will be constantly trembling, constantly afraid, in fear.

Have you not watched the so-called religious people? They are always afraid— afraid of hell—and always trying to get into

heaven. But they don't know what heaven is; they have not tasted it at all. If you change your consciousness, heaven comes to you, not that you go to heaven. Nobody has ever gone to heaven, and nobody has ever gone to hell. Let it be decided once and for all: heaven comes to you, hell comes to you—it depends on you. Whatsoever you call, it comes.

If your being changes, you suddenly become available to heaven—heaven descends on you. If your being does not change, you are in a conflict; you are forcing something that is not there. You become false and more false, until you become two persons, you become schizophrenic, split. You show one thing, but you are something else. You say something but you never do it; instead, you do something else. You are continuously playing hide-and-seek with yourself. Anxiety and anguish are natural in such a state—that's what hell is.

understanding the
science of tantra

Tantra is science, not philosophy. To understand philosophy

is easy because only your intellect is required. If you can

understand language, if you can understand concept,

you can understand philosophy. You need not change;

no transformation is required of you. As you are, you can

understand philosophy—but not Tantra. To understand Tantra

you will need a change... rather, a mutation. Unless you are

willing to undergo a mutation you will not understand, because

Tantra is not an intellectual proposition, it is an experience.

Only when you are receptive, ready, and vulnerable to the

experience, is it going to come to you.

the language of silence

We have lost contact with existence; we have lost our roots in it. We are like an uprooted tree—the sap flows no more, the juice has dried up. No more flowers will bloom, no more fruits will ripen. Not even birds come to take shelter in us. This happens because we are not yet born. We have taken the physical birth to be our birth—it is not our birth. We exist only as potentialities; we have not become actual— hence our misery. The actual is blissful, the potential *is miserable. Why is it so? Because the potential cannot be at rest. The potential is continuously restless—it has to be restless! Something is going to happen and it hangs in the air. We are in limbo.*

It is like a seed—how can a seed rest and relax? Rest and relaxation is known only by the flowers. The seed has to be deep in anguish; the seed has to continuously tremble. The trembling is because it does not know whether it will be able to become actual, whether it will find the right soil, whether it will find the right climate, whether it will find the right sky. Is it going to happen, or will it simply die without ever being born? The seed trembles inside. The seed has anxiety, anguish. The seed cannot sleep; the seed suffers from insomnia.

The potential is ambitious. The potential longs for the future. Have you not watched this in your own being? You are continuously longing for something to happen and it is not happening; you are continuously hankering, hoping, desiring, dreaming... and it is not happening! Life goes on flowing by. Life goes on slipping out of your hands. Death comes closer, and you are not yet actual. Who knows? Which will come first? Actualization, realization, blossoming, or maybe death? Who knows? Hence the fear, the anguish, the trembling.

Soren Kierkegaard has said man is a trembling. Yes, man is a trembling because man is a seed. Friedrich Nietzsche has said man is a bridge. Exactly right! Man is not a place to rest; he is a bridge to pass over. Man is a door to go through. You cannot rest at being human. Man is not yet a *being*; man is an arrow on the way, a rope stretched between two eternities. Man is a tension. Only humans suffer from anxiety—we are the only animals on the earth that suffer from anxiety. What can be the cause of it?

It is only humans who exist as potentiality. A dog is actual; there is nothing else waiting to

happen. A buffalo is actual; there is nothing more, it has already happened. Whatever could happen, has happened. You cannot say to a buffalo, "You are not yet a buffalo." That would be foolish. But you can say to a man, "You are not yet a man." You can say to a woman, "You are incomplete." You cannot say to a dog, "You are incomplete." That would be stupid. All dogs are fully complete.

The human being has a possibility, a future. The human being is an opening. So there is a constant fear: Are we going to make it or not? How many times have we missed before? Are we going to miss again? That's why we are not happy. Existence goes on celebrating, there is great singing, there is great joy, there is great rejoicing! The whole of existence is always in an orgy; it is a carnival. The whole of existence at each moment is in orgasm! But somehow the human being has become a stranger.

Humans have forgotten the language of innocence. Humans have forgotten how to relate with existence. Humans have forgotten how to relate with themselves!

To relate with yourself is meditation and to relate with existence is prayer. People have forgotten the very language. That's why we appear like strangers in our own home, strangers to ourselves. We don't know who we are and we don't know why we are, and we don't know for what we go on existing. It seems to be an endless waiting... waiting for Godot.

Nobody knows whether Godot is ever going to come or not. In fact, who is this Godot? Nobody knows even that, but you have to wait for something, so you create some idea and wait for it. God is that idea. Heaven is that idea. Nirvana is that idea. You have to wait because

you have to fill your being, otherwise you feel so empty. Waiting gives a sense of purpose and a direction. You can feel better because at least you are waiting. It has not happened yet but it is going to happen some day.

What is it that is going to happen? We have not even asked the right question—and remember, once the right question is asked, the right answer is not far away. It is just around the corner. In fact, it is hidden within the right question itself. If you ask the right question, you will find the right answer through that questioning itself.

The first thing that I would like to say is that we are continually missing, because we have used the mind as the language to relate with existence and the mind is a way to cut yourself off from existence. It is the way to set yourself apart; it is not the way to turn yourself on. *Thinking is the barrier*. Thoughts are like the Great Wall of China around you, and when you are groping through the thoughts you cannot touch reality. Not that reality is far away—it is always close by, just a prayer away at the most. But if you are thinking, brooding, analyzing, interpreting, or philosophizing, then you start falling farther and farther away from reality. The more thoughts you have, the more difficult it is to see through them. They create a great fog; they create blindness.

This is another fundamental of Tantra: a thinking mind is a mind that misses; thinking is not the language to relate with reality. Then what is the language to relate with reality? Non-thinking. Words are meaningless with reality. Silence is meaningful. Silence is pregnant; words are dead. You have to learn the language of silence.

You were in your mother's womb—you have forgotten it completely, but for nine months you had not yet spoken a single word—you were together, in deep silence. You were one with your mother; there was no barrier between you and your mother. You didn't exist as a separate self. In that deep silence, your mother and you were one. There was tremendous unity—not union—unity. You were not two, so it was not union—it was simple unity.

The day you become silent again, the same thing happens: again you fall into the womb of existence; again you relate. You relate in a totally new way. Not quite *totally* new, because you knew it in your mother's womb, but you have forgotten it. That's what I mean when I say humans have forgotten the language to relate. That is the way—as you related with your mother in her womb. Your every vibe was conveyed to your mother; every vibe of your mother was conveyed to you. There was a simple understanding; no misunderstanding existed between you and your mother. Misunderstanding comes only when thinking comes in.

How can you misunderstand somebody without thinking? Can you? Can you misunderstand me if you don't think about me? How can you misunderstand? And how can you understand me if you think? Impossible—the moment you think, you have started interpreting. The moment you think, you are not looking at me; you are avoiding me. You are hiding behind your thoughts. Your thoughts come from your past. I am here, present. I am a statement here and now, and you bring your past.

You must know about the squid. When it wants to hide, it releases a cloud of black ink around itself. Then nobody can see it. It is simply lost in its cloud of black ink; the cloud is its safety measure. Exactly the same thing is happening when you release a cloud of thoughts around you—you become lost in it. Then you cannot relate and nobody can relate to you.

It is impossible to relate to a mind; you can relate only to a consciousness. A consciousness has no past. A mind is just past and nothing else.

So Tantra says you have to learn the language of orgasm. Again, when you are making love to a woman or to a man, what happens? For a few seconds—it is very rare and becoming even rarer as humans become more and more civilized—for a few seconds, you are no longer in the mind. With a shock, you are cut off from the mind. In a leap, you are outside the mind. For those few seconds of orgasm when you are out of the mind, you can relate. Again you are back in the womb… in the womb of your woman or in the womb of your man. You are no longer separate. Again there is unity, not union. When you start making love, there is the beginning of a union. But when orgasm comes, there is no union—there is unity. The duality is lost.

What happens in that deep, peak experience? Tantra reminds you again and again that whatever happens in that peak moment is the language to relate with existence. It is the language of the guts; it is the language of your very being. So either think in terms of when you were in the womb of your mother, or think in terms of when you are lost in the womb of your beloved and, for a few seconds, the mind simply does not work! Those moments of no-mind are your glimpses into eternity, glimpses of awakening, glimpses of the beyond. We have forgotten that language and that language has to be learned again.

> " Learn the language of love, the language of silence, the language of each other's presence. "

Love is the language. The language of love is silent. When two lovers are in deep harmony, or what Carl Jung used to call synchronicity— when their vibes are synchronizing with each other and they are both vibrating on the same wavelength—then there is silence. Then the lovers don't need to talk. It is only husbands and wives who talk. Lovers fall silent.

In fact, the husband and wife cannot keep silent because language is a way to avoid each other. If you are not avoiding the other, if you are not talking, the presence of the other becomes embarrassing. So the husband and wife immediately release their cloud of black ink! Any excuse will do, but they release ink around themselves; they get lost in the cloud, then there is no problem.

Language is not a way to relate more or less, it is a way to avoid. When you are deeply in love you may hold the hand of your beloved but you will be in silence… utter silence, not a ripple. In that rippleless lake of your consciousness, something is conveyed, the message is given. It is a wordless message.

Tantra says you have to learn the language of love, the language of silence, the language of each other's presence, the language of the heart, the language of the guts. We have learned a language that is not existential. We have learned an alien language—utilitarian, of course; it fulfills a certain purpose. But as far as the higher exploration of consciousness is concerned, it is a barrier.

On the lower level it is okay—in the marketplace you need a certain language; silence won't do. But as you move deeper and higher, language won't do.

tantra and yoga

Tantra and yoga are basically different. They reach the same goal; however, their paths are not only different, but contrary. This has to be understood clearly.

The yoga process is also methodology; yoga is also technique. Yoga is not philosophy; just like Tantra, yoga depends on action, method, technique. Doing leads to being in yoga also, but the process is different. In yoga one has to fight; it is the path of the warrior. On the path of Tantra one does not have to fight at all. On the contrary, one has to indulge, but with awareness.

Yoga is suppression with awareness; Tantra is indulgence with awareness. Tantra says that whatsoever you are, the ultimate is not opposite to it. It is a process of growth; you can grow to be the ultimate. There is no opposition between you and reality. You are part of it, so no struggle, no conflict, no opposition to nature is needed. You have to use nature; you have to use whatsoever you are to go beyond.

In yoga you have to fight with yourself to go beyond. In yoga, the world and *moksha*, liberation—you as you are, and you are as you can be—are two opposite things. Suppress, fight, dissolve that which you are so you can attain that which you can be. Going beyond is a death in yoga. You must die for your real being to be born. In the eyes of Tantra, yoga is suicide. You must kill your natural self—your body, your instincts, your desires, everything. Tantra says accept yourself as you are. It is a deep acceptance. Do not create a gap between you and the real, between the world and Nirvana. Do not create any gap. There is no gap for Tantra; no death is needed. For your rebirth, no death is needed—rather, a transcendence is required. For this transcendence, use yourself.

For example, sex is there: the basic energy you are born through, born with. The basic cells of your being and of your body are sexual, so the human mind revolves around sex. For yoga you must fight with this energy. Through fighting you create a different center in yourself. The more you fight, the more you become integrated in a different center. Then sex is not your center. Fighting with sex—of course, consciously—will create in you a new center of being, a new emphasis, and a new crystallization. Then sex will not be your energy. You will create your energy fighting with sex. A different energy will come into being and a different center of existence.

For Tantra you have to use the energy of sex. Do not fight with it, transform it. Do not think in terms of enmity, be friendly to it. It is your energy. It is not evil; it is not bad. Every energy

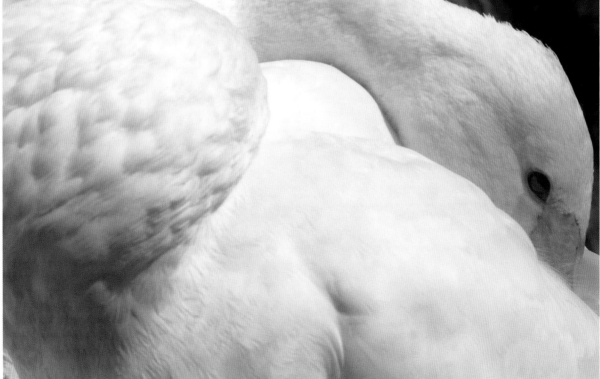

is natural. It can be used for you or it can be used against you. You can make a block or a barrier of it, or you can make it a step. Rightly used, it becomes friendly; wrongly used, it becomes your enemy. But it is neither. Energy is just natural. As ordinary people are using sex, it becomes an enemy. It destroys; they dissipate in it.

Yoga takes the opposite view—opposite to the ordinary mind. The ordinary mind is being destroyed by its own desires, so yoga says stop desiring, be desireless. Fight desire and create an integration in you that is desireless.

Tantra teaches you to be aware of the desire; do not create any fight. Move in desire with full consciousness, and when you move into desire with full consciousness, you will transcend it. You are into it and still you are not in it. You pass through it, but you remain an outsider.

Yoga has much appeal because yoga is the opposite of the ordinary mind, so the ordinary mind can understand the language of yoga. You know how sex is destroying you—how it has destroyed you, how you revolve around it like a slave, like a puppet. You know this by your experience. So when yoga says fight it, you immediately understand the language. That is the appeal, the easy appeal of yoga.

Tantra cannot be so easily appealing. It seems difficult: How to move into desire without being overwhelmed by it? How to be in the sex act consciously, with full awareness? The

ordinary mind becomes afraid. It seems dangerous. Not that it is dangerous; whatsoever you know about sex creates this danger for you. You know yourself, you know how you can deceive yourself. You know very well that your mind is cunning. You can move in desire, in sex, in everything, and you can deceive yourself that you are moving with full awareness. That is why you feel the danger.

The danger is not in Tantra; it is in you. The appeal of yoga is because of you, because of your ordinary mind—your sex-suppressed, sex-starved, sex-indulging mind. Because the ordinary mind is not healthy about sex, yoga has an appeal. With a better humanity, with a healthy sex—natural, normal—the case would be different. We are not normal and natural. We are absolutely abnormal, unhealthy, insane. But because everyone is like us, we never feel it.

Madness is so normal that not to be mad may look abnormal. A Buddha seems abnormal. A Jesus is abnormal amidst us. They do not belong to us. Our "normalcy" is a disease. This "normal" mind has created the appeal of yoga. If you take sex naturally—with no philosophy around it, either for or against—if you take sex as you take your hands or your eyes, as accepted and natural, then Tantra will have an appeal. Only then can Tantra be useful for many.

But the days of Tantra are coming. Sooner or later Tantra will explode for the first time in the masses, because for the first time the time is ripe—ripe to take sex naturally. It is possible that the explosion may come from the West, because Freud, Jung, and Reich have prepared the background. They did not know anything about Tantra, but they have prepared the basic ground for Tantra to evolve. Western psychology has come to the conclusion that the basic human disease is related to sex, the basic insanity of man is sex-oriented.

Unless this sex orientation is dissolved, people cannot be natural and normal. Humans have gone wrong only because of the prevailing attitudes about sex. No attitude is needed. Only then are you natural. What attitude have you about your eyes? Are they evil or are they divine? Are you for your eyes or against them? There is no attitude! That is why your eyes are normal.

Take an attitude—think that eyes are evil. Then seeing will become difficult. Seeing will take the same problematic shape that sex has taken. Then you will want to see, you will desire and you will hanker to see. But when you see, you will feel guilty. Whenever you see, you will feel that you have done something wrong, that you have sinned. You would like to kill your very instrument of seeing; you would like to destroy your eyes. And the more you want to destroy them, the more you will become eye-centered. Then you will begin an absurd activity. You will want to see more and more, and simultaneously you will feel more and more guilty. The same phenomenon has happened with the sex center.

Tantra says, Accept whatsoever you are. This is the basic note—total acceptance. Only through total acceptance can you grow. Then use every energy you have. How can you use them? Accept them, then find out what these energies are—what is sex, what is this phenomenon? We are not acquainted with it. We know many things about sex, taught by others. We may have passed through the sex act, but with a guilty mind, a suppressive attitude, in haste, in a hurry. Something has to be done in order to become unburdened. The sex act is not a loving act. You are not happy in it, but you cannot leave it. The more you try to leave it, the more attractive it becomes. The more you want to negate it, the more you feel invited.

You cannot negate it, but this tendency to negate and destroy destroys the mind, the awareness, the sensitivity that can understand it. So sex goes on with no sensitivity in it. Then you cannot understand it. Only a deep sensitivity can understand anything; only a deep feeling, a deep moving into it, can understand anything. You can understand sex only if you move in it as a poet moves amidst flowers—only then! If you feel guilty about flowers, you may pass through the garden, but you will pass with closed eyes. And you will be in a hurry, in a deep, mad haste. Somehow you have to go out of the garden. Then how can you be aware?

So Tantra says, accept whatsoever you are. You are a great mystery of many multi-dimensional energies. Accept it, and move with every energy with deep sensitivity, with awareness, with love, with understanding. Move with it! Then every desire becomes a vehicle to go beyond it. Then every energy becomes a help. Then this world becomes Nirvana, this body becomes a temple—a holy temple, a holy place.

Yoga is negation; Tantra is affirmation. Yoga is defined in terms of duality—that is the reason for the word *yoga*. It means to put two things together, to "yoke" two things together. But two things are there; the duality is there. Tantra says there is no duality. If there is duality, then you cannot put them together. Howsoever you try, they will remain two and the fight will continue, the dualism will remain.

If the world and the divine are two, then they cannot be put together. If they are not two, if they only *appear* as two, only then can they be one. If your body and your soul are two, then they cannot be put together. If you and God are two, then there is no possibility of putting you together. You will remain two.

Tantra says there is no duality; it is only an appearance. So why help this appearance of duality to grow stronger? Dissolve it this very moment! Be one! Through acceptance you become one, not through fight. Accept the world, accept the body, accept everything that is inherent in it. Do not create a different center in yourself, because for Tantra that different center is nothing but the ego. Do not create an ego. Just be aware of what you are. If you fight, then the ego will be there.

It is difficult to find a yogi who is not an egoist. And yogis may go on talking about egolessness, but they cannot be egoless. The very process they go through creates the ego. The fight is the process. If you fight, you are bound to create an ego. And the more you fight, the more strengthened the ego will be. If you win your fight, then you will achieve the supreme ego.

Tantra says, no fight! Then there is no possibility of ego. If we understand Tantra, there will be many problems because, for us, if there is no fight there is only indulgence. No fight means indulgence for us. Then we become afraid. We have indulged for lives together and we have reached nowhere. But in Tantra, indulgence is not "our" indulgence. Tantra says, Indulge, but be aware.

You are angry... Tantra will not say, Do not be angry. Tantra will say, Be angry wholeheartedly, but be aware. Tantra is not against anger. Tantra is only against spiritual sleepiness, spiritual unconsciousness. Be aware *and* be angry. And this is the secret of the method: if you are aware, anger is transformed; it becomes compassion. So according to Tantra, anger is not your enemy; it is compassion in seed form. The same anger, the same energy, will become compassion.

If you fight with your anger, then there will be no possibility of compassion. If you succeed in fighting, in suppression, you will be dead. There will be no anger because you have suppressed it, but there will be no compassion either, because only anger can be transformed into compassion.

If you succeed in your suppression—which is impossible—then there will be no sex, but no love either, because with sex dead there is no energy to grow into love. So you will be without sex, and you will also be without love. And then the whole point is missed, because without love there is no divineness, without love there is no liberation, and without love there is no freedom.

Tantra says that these same energies are to be transformed. It can be said in this way: if you are against the world, then there is no Nirvana, because this world itself is to be transformed

into Nirvana. Then you are against the basic energies that are the source.

So Tantric alchemy says, Do not fight, be friendly with all the energies that are given to you. Welcome them. Feel grateful that you have anger, that you have sex, that you have greed. Feel grateful because these are the hidden sources and they can be transformed, they can be opened. When sex is transformed it becomes love. The poison is lost and the ugliness is lost.

The seed is ugly, but when it becomes alive it sprouts and flowers. Then there is beauty. Do not throw away the seed, because then you are also throwing away the flowers in it. They are not yet manifest so that you can see them. They are unmanifest, but they are there. Use this seed so that you can attain flowers. So first let there be acceptance, a sensitive understanding and awareness. Then indulgence is allowed.

One thing more which, although strange, is one of the deepest discoveries of Tantra, and that is: Whatsoever you take as your enemies— greed, anger, hate, sex—your attitude that they are enemies makes them your enemies. Take them as divine gifts and approach them with a grateful heart.

For Tantra, everything is holy. Remember this: for Tantra, *everything* is holy, nothing is unholy. For an irreligious person, everything is unholy and for so-called religious persons something is holy and something else is unholy. Tantra says everything is holy, that is why we cannot understand it. It is the deepest non-dual standpoint—if we can call it a standpoint. Because any standpoint is bound to be dual and Tantra is not against anything, it is not any standpoint. It is a felt unity, a lived unity.

These are two paths, yoga and Tantra. Tantra could not be as appealing because of our crippled minds. But for someone who is healthy inside, not in chaos, Tantra has a beauty. Only such a person can understand what Tantra is. Yoga has an easy appeal because of our disturbed minds. Remember, it is ultimately your mind that makes anything attractive or unattractive. You are the deciding factor.

the inner map
of the chakras

Tantra has a certain map of the inner man. It will be good if you understand that map, as it will help you. Both Tantra and yoga suppose that there are seven centers in human physiology—the subtle physiology, not the material physiology of the body. In fact, these centers are metaphors, but they are helpful in understanding something of the inner being. These are the seven chakras.

First and most basic is *muladhar*, which means the most fundamental or basic. *Mul* means "of the roots." The muladhar chakra is the center where sex energy is, but society has badly damaged that chakra.

This muladhar chakra has three aspects to it: one is oral; the second is anal, and the third is genital. These are the three aspects of the muladhar. The child begins his life in the oral, and because of wrong upbringing many people remain at the oral stage; they never grow beyond it. That's why there is so much smoking, chewing gum, constantly eating. This is an oral fixation: these people remain centered in the mouth.

There are many primitive societies in which partners don't kiss. In fact, if the child has grown well, kissing will disappear. Kissing shows the person has remained oral. Otherwise, what does sex have to do with lips? When for the first time primitive societies came to know about civilized man's kissing, they laughed. They simply thought it ridiculous. Two persons kissing each other? It seems unhygienic too: transferring all sorts of illnesses and infections to each other. What are they doing and why? But most of humanity has remained oral.

If the child is not satisfied orally—the mother does not give her breast as much as the child needs—the lips remain unsatisfied. So the child will grow up to smoke cigarettes, become a great kisser, chew gum, or become a great eater, continually eating this or that. If mothers give their breasts as much as the children need, then the muladhar is not damaged.

If you are a smoker, try a pacifier—and you will be suddenly surprised. It has helped many people. I suggest it to many people. If somebody asks me how to stop smoking, I say, "Just get a pacifier and keep it in your mouth. Let it hang around your neck and whenever you feel like smoking, just put the pacifier in your mouth and enjoy it. Within three weeks you will be surprised: the urge to smoke has disappeared."

Somewhere in the psyche the breast is still appealing. That's why men are so focused on breasts. There seems to be no reason why.

Why are men so interested in breasts? Painting, sculpture, film, pornography—everything seems to be breast-oriented! And women are always trying to hide and yet show their breasts; otherwise, the bra is just foolish. It is a trick to hide and to exhibit together; it is a contradictory trick. And now they are stuffing breasts with silicon so they become bigger and can take on the shape that un-grown-up humanity wants to see. Such a childish idea! But humanity remains oral.

This is the lowest state of the muladhar.

A few people change from oral and become stuck at anal, because the second great damage happens with toilet training. Children are forced to go to the toilet at a certain time. Young children cannot control their bowel movements; it takes time, it takes years for them to develop control. So what do they do? They force themselves, they close their anal mechanism, and because of this they become anally fixated.

That's why so much constipation exists in the world. Only humans suffer from constipation.

In the wild state, no animal suffers from constipation. Constipation is more psychological; it is the result of damage to the muladhar. Because of constipation many other things develop in the human mind. A person becomes a hoarder—a hoarder of knowledge, of money, of virtue—and becomes miserly. He cannot let go of anything! Whatever he grabs, he holds on to it. With this anal emphasis, great damage happens to the muladhar. When things develop naturally, the man or the woman will move on to the genital. If people get fixated at the oral or at the anal, they never move on to the genital— that is the trick that society has used until now not to allow you to become fully sexual. The anal fixation becomes so important that the genitals become less important.

Finally, some people become genital—if somehow they are not fixated at the oral and the anal—and then guilt is created in humanity about sex. Sex is equivalent to sin. Christianity has considered sex so much a sin that they go on trying to prove the foolish idea that Christ was born out of a miracle, that he was not born out of a man-woman relationship, but that Mary was a virgin. Sex is such a sin… how could Jesus' mother have sex? It is okay for ordinary people, but for Jesus' mother to have sex… how could Jesus, such a pure man, be born out of sex?

Sex has been condemned so much that you cannot enjoy it. That's why energy remains fixated somewhere else, whether oral, anal, or genital. It cannot go upward.

Tantra says that the first great work has to happen in the muladhar. For oral freedom, screaming, laughing, shouting, crying, and weeping are all helpful. That's why I emphasize cathartic methods of meditation—they help to relieve the oral fixation. To relieve you of the anal fixation, fast, chaotic breathing is helpful because it hits directly on the anal center and enables you to relax the anal mechanism. Here the Dynamic Meditation is of tremendous value.

DYNAMIC MEDITATION

OSHO DYNAMIC MEDITATION is an hour-long process consisting of five stages: (1) vigorous, chaotic breathing; (2) catharsis; (3) grounding and centering; (4) silent watchfulness; and (5) celebration through dance. Osho developed the meditation specifically for modern men and women, and guided the composition of music to support each stage in the process. For more detailed instructions and information about where to find the music, see www.osho.com/dynamic

Then the sex center has to be relieved of the burden of guilt and condemnation. You have to learn about it all over again; only then can the damaged sex center function in a healthy way. You have to relearn it to enjoy it without any guilt.

There are a thousand and one types of guilt. In the Hindu mind, there is a fear that semen represents a great energy—if even a single drop is lost, you are lost. This is a constipated attitude —hoard the semen so nothing is lost! But you are such a dynamic force that, in fact, you create that energy every day. Nothing is lost.

The Hindu mind is too obsessed with *veerya*, with semen energy. Since not a single drop should be lost, they are continuously afraid. Whenever they make love—if they make love—then they feel frustrated and depressed, because they start thinking so much energy has been lost.

Nothing is lost. You don't have a fixed quota of energy. You are a dynamo. You create energy; you create it each day. In fact, the more you use it, the more you have it. It functions like the rest of the body. If you use your muscles, they will grow. If you walk, your legs will be strong. If you run, you will have more energy to run. Don't think that a person who has never run and suddenly runs will have energy—he will not have energy. He will not have even the musculature to run. Use all that has been given to you by nature and you will have more of it.

The Hindu madness, to hoard, is on the lines of constipation. There is an American madness that is like diarrhea: just throw everything out, meaningfully or meaninglessly, go on squandering your energy and indulging. Even a man of eighty years still thinks in childish ways.

Sex is good, sex is beautiful, but it is not the end. It is the alpha but not the omega. You have to go beyond it. But to say that you have to go beyond it is not a condemnation! You have to go *through* it to go beyond it.

Tantra is the healthiest attitude about sex. It says sex is good, sex is healthy, sex is natural, and sex has more possibilities than just reproduction. Sex has more possibilities than just fun. Sex carries something of the ultimate in it, something of *samadhi*, of transcendence.

The muladhar chakra has to be relaxed— relaxed from constipation, relaxed from diarrhea. The muladhar chakra has to function at the optimum, one hundred percent, then energy starts moving.

The second chakra is *svadhisthan*—that is, the *hara*, the death center. These first two centers are both damaged because man has been afraid of sex and man has been afraid of death. Death has been avoided: don't talk about death, just forget about it! It does not exist. Even if sometimes it happens, don't take any note of it. Go on thinking that you will live forever—avoid death.

Tantra says: Don't avoid sex and don't avoid death. That's why Saraha went to the cremation ground to meditate—not to avoid death. And he went with the arrowsmith woman to live a life of healthy, full sex, of optimum sex. On the cremation ground, living with a woman, these two centers had to be relaxed: the center of death and the center of sex. Once you accept death and are not afraid of it, once you accept sex and are not afraid of it, your two lower centers are relaxed.

Those are the two lower centers that have been damaged by society, badly damaged. Once they are relieved, the other five centers are accessible. They are not damaged. There has been no need to damage them because people don't live in those other five centers.

These two centers are naturally available—birth has happened, the sex center, muladhar. And death is going to happen—the second center, svadhisthan. These two things are in everyone's life, so society has destroyed both centers and tried to manipulate people, to dominate them through these two centers.

Tantra says: Meditate while you make love. Meditate while somebody dies—go, watch, see. Sit by the side of a dying man. Feel, participate in his death. Go in deep meditation with the dying man. When a man is dying, there is the possibility of having a taste of death—because when a man is dying, he releases so much energy from the svadhisthan chakra. The whole repressed energy of the svadhisthan chakra will be released as he is dying. Without releasing it, he will not be able to die.

So when a man dies or a woman dies, don't miss the opportunity. If you are close to a dying person, sit silently, meditate silently. When the person dies, in a sudden burst the energy will be all around and you can taste death. It will give you a great sense of relaxation: you will experience that, yes, death happens, but nobody dies. Yes, death happens, but in fact death *never* happens.

While making love, meditate so that you can know that something of samadhi penetrates into sexuality. While meditating on death, go deep into it so that you can see that something of the deathless enters into death. These two experiences will help you to go upward very easily.

The other five centers, fortunately, are not destroyed; they are perfectly in tune—only the energy has to be freed to move through them. If the first two centers are helped to relax, energy starts moving. So let death and love be your two objects of meditation.

Muladhar means the base, the root. It is the sex center, or you can call it the life center, the birth center. It is from muladhar that you are born. It is from your mother's muladhar and your father's muladhar that you have come into your body. The death chakra is *svadhisthan*: it means "the abode of the self."

This is a very strange name to give to the death chakra—"abode of the self," svadhisthan, where you really exist. In death? Yes. When you die, you come to your pure existence—because the only part of you that dies is that which you are not. The body dies—the body is born out of the muladhar. When you die the body disappears, but do you? No. Whatever has been given by the muladhar is taken away by svadhisthan. Your mother and father have given you a certain mechanism of the body—that is taken away in death. But *you*? You existed even before your father and mother knew each other; you have existed always.

Somebody asks Jesus about Abraham, what he thinks about the prophet Abraham, and he says: "Abraham? I am before Abraham ever was." Abraham lived almost two thousand, three thousand years before Jesus, and he says, "I am before Abraham was." What is he talking about? As far as bodies are concerned, how can he

exist before Abraham? He is not talking about the body—he is talking about "I-am-ness," his pure being. That pure being is eternal.

So this name, *svadhisthan*, is beautiful. It is exactly the center that in Japan is known as the *hara*. That's why in Japan suicide is called *harakiri*—to kill yourself through the hara center. The svadhisthan takes only that which has been given by the muladhar. But that which has come from eternity, your consciousness, is not taken away.

Hindus have been great explorers of consciousness. They called this center svadhisthan because when you die, then you know who you are. Die in love and you will know who you are. Die in meditation and you will know who you are. Die to the past and you will know who you are. Die to the mind and you will know who you are. Death is the way to know.

These two centers have been poisoned by society because these are the centers easily

 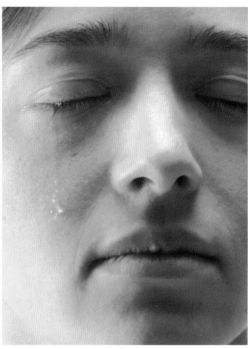

available to society. Beyond these two are five more centers.

The third center, *manipura*, is the center of all your sentiments, emotions. It means the diamond—life is valuable because of sentiments, emotions, laughter, crying, tears, and smiles. Life is valuable because of all these things. These are the glory of life—hence the chakra is called manipura, the diamond chakra.

Only humans are capable of having this precious diamond. Animals cannot laugh; naturally, they cannot cry either. Tears are a certain dimension that is available only to humans. The beauty of tears, the beauty of laughter; the poetry of tears, and the poetry of laughter are available to humans only. All other animals exist with only two chakras: muladhar and svadhisthan. They are born and they die. If you are also born and you die, and nothing else happens, you are like an animal—you are not

human yet. Yet many millions of people exist only with these two chakras; they never go beyond them.

We repress our emotions in the manipura. We have been taught to repress sentiments. We have been taught that sentimentality does not pay—be practical, be hard; don't be soft, don't be vulnerable; otherwise, you will be exploited. Be hard! At least *show* that you are hard, at least pretend that you are dangerous, that you are not a soft being. Create fear around you. Don't laugh—if you laugh you cannot create fear around you. Don't weep—if you weep you show that you are afraid. Don't show your human limitations; pretend that you are perfect.

Much work is done in Tantra to relax this third center. Emotions have to be relieved, relaxed. When you feel like crying you must cry; when you feel like laughing you must laugh. You

must drop this nonsense of repression, you have to learn expression, because only through your sentiments, your emotions, and your sensitivity, do you come to that vibration through which communication is possible.

Have you not seen it? You can say as much as you want, and nothing is said; but a tear rolls down your cheek and everything is said. A tear can say much more. You can talk for hours and it won't do, yet a tear can say all. You can say, "I am happy," but a little laughter—real, authentic laughter—and you need not say anything; the laughter says it all. When you see your friend, your face beams, flashes with joy.

The third center has to be made more and more available. It is against thinking, so if you allow the third center, you will relax in your tense mind more easily. Be authentic, sensitive: touch more, feel more, laugh more, cry more. Remember, you cannot do more than is needed;

> **❝ You cannot laugh more than is needed. So don't be afraid and don't be miserly. ❞**

you cannot exaggerate. You cannot even bring a single tear more than is needed, and you cannot laugh more than is needed. So don't be afraid and don't be miserly.

Tantra allows life all its emotions.

These are the three lower centers—lower but not in any sense of valuation—these are the three lower rungs of the ladder.

Then comes the fourth center, the heart center, called *anahata*. The word is beautiful.

Anahata means "unstruck sound." It is exactly what Zen people mean when they say, "Do you hear the sound of one hand clapping?" Unstruck sound.

The heart is in the middle—three centers below it, three centers above it. The heart is the door from the lower to the higher, or from the higher to the lower. The heart is like a crossroad.

The heart has been completely bypassed. You have not been taught to be heartful. You have not even been allowed to go into the realm of the heart, because it is very dangerous. It is the center of the soundless sound, the unstruck sound, the non-linguistic center. Language is struck sound: we have to create it with our vocal chords. Language is two hands clapping. The heart is one hand clapping. In the heart there is no word; it is wordless.

We have avoided the heart completely; we have bypassed it. We move in such a way in our being as if the heart does not exist—or, at the most, as if it is only a pumping mechanism for breathing. It is not. The lungs are not the heart. The heart is hidden deep behind the lungs. And it is not physical either. It is the place from which love arises.

That's why love is not a sentiment. Sentimental love belongs to the third center, not to the fourth. Love is not just sentimental. Love has more depth than sentiment; love has more validity than sentiment. Sentiments are momentary.

More or less, the sentiment of love is misunderstood as the experience of love. One day you fall in love with a man or a woman, and the next day it is gone—and you call it love. It is not love, it is a sentiment. You liked the man—

liked, remember, not *loved*—it was a "liking" just as you like ice cream. Likings come and go. Likings are momentary; they cannot stay long; they don't have any capacity to stay long. You liked a man, you made love with him, and finished! The liking is finished. Just as you liked ice cream—you have eaten it and now you don't look at the ice cream at all. And if somebody gives you more ice cream, you will say, "Now it is making me sick—stop! I cannot take any more."

Liking is not love. Never misunderstand liking for love, otherwise your whole life you will be only driftwood... you will be drifting from one person to another and intimacy will never grow.

The fourth center, the anahata, is significant because it is through the heart that you were first related to your mother. It was through the heart that you were related to your mother, not through the head. In deep love, in deep orgasm, again you are related through the heart, not through the head. In meditation, in prayer, the same thing happens: you are related with existence through the heart—heart-to-heart. Yes, it is a dialogue heart-to-heart, not head-to-head. It is non-linguistic.

The heart center is the center from which the soundless sound arises. If you relax into the heart center, you will hear it. That is a great discovery. Those who have entered the heart hear a continuous chanting inside their being which sounds like *aum*. Have you ever heard anything like a chanting that goes on by itself, not that you are *doing* it?

That's why I am not in favor of mantras. You can continuously chant *aum, aum, aum,* and create a mental substitute for the heart. It is not going to help you. It is a deception. You can

chant for years and create a false sound within yourself as if your heart is speaking—it is not.

To know the heart you are not to chant *aum* —you have only to be silent. One day, suddenly, the mantra is there. One day, when you have fallen silent, you will hear the sound coming from nowhere. It is arising out of you from the innermost core. It is the sound of your inner silence. Just as in a silent night there is a certain sound, the sound of silence, exactly like that but on a much deeper level, a sound arises in you.

It arises—let me remind you again and again—it is not that you bring it in; it is not that you repeat *aum*, *aum*. No, you don't say a single word. You are simply quiet. You are silent. It bursts forth like a spring… suddenly it starts flowing… it is there. You hear it—you don't say it—you hear it.

When Mohammedans say that Mohammed *heard* the Koran, that is their meaning. That is exactly what happens at the innermost core of your heart. Not that you say it, but that you *hear* it. Mohammed heard the Koran—he heard it happening inside. He was puzzled; he had never heard anything like this. It was so unknown, so unfamiliar. The story says that he became ill. If one day, while sitting in your room, you suddenly start hearing inside *aum*, *aum* (or

anything else) you will start to wonder, "Am I going mad?" You are not saying it, nobody else is saying it... are you going mad?

Mohammed was sitting on a hilltop when he heard it. He came home trembling and perspiring with a high fever. He became disturbed. He told his wife, "Bring all the blankets and cover me! I have never had such a trembling. A great fever has come to me," But his wife could see that his face was illuminated.

"What type of fever is this? His eyes are burning, afire with something tremendously beautiful. A grace has entered with him into the house. A great silence has fallen over the house." Then his wife started hearing something. She said to Mohammed, "I don't think it is a fever—I think God has blessed you. Don't be afraid! What has happened? Tell me!"

His wife was the first Mohammedan—Khadija was her name. She was the first convert. She said, "I can see—God has happened to you, something is flowing from your heart all over the place. You have become luminous! You have never been like this—something extraordinary has happened. Tell me why you are so worried and trembling. Maybe it feels strange, but tell me."

So Mohammed told her, afraid of what she would think, but she became converted—she was the first Mohammedan.

It has happened so always. Hindus say that the Vedas were recited by God himself. It simply means that they were *heard*. In India, we have a word for the holy scriptures: the word is *shruti* and it means "that which has been heard."

At the center of the heart, in the anahata chakra, you hear. But if you have not heard

> *The waterfall is there, and the sound of running water is there, but you have avoided it, you have bypassed it.*

anything inside you—no sound, no aum, no mantra—that simply means you have avoided the heart. The waterfall is there, and the sound of running water is there, but you have avoided it, you have bypassed it. You have taken some other route; you have taken a shortcut avoiding the fourth center. The fourth is the most dangerous center because it is the center out of which trust and faith are born, and the mind wants to avoid it. If the mind does not avoid it, then there will be no possibility for doubt. Mind lives through doubt.

This is the fourth center. And Tantra says, Through love you will come to know this fourth center.

The fifth center is called *visuddhi*, which means "purity." Certainly, after love has happened, there is purity and innocence—never before it. Only love purifies—*only* love—nothing else purifies. Even the homeliest person in love becomes beautiful. Love is nectar. It cleanses all poisons. So the fifth chakra is purity, absolute purity. It is the throat center.

Tantra says: Only speak when you have come to the fifth center via the fourth—only speak through love; otherwise, don't speak.

Speak through compassion; otherwise, don't speak! What is point of speaking? If you have come through the heart and if you have heard existence speaking there, or existence running there like a waterfall, or if you have heard the sound of existence in the sound of one hand clapping, then you are allowed to speak. Then your throat center can convey the message, then something can be poured into words. When you *have* it, it can be poured even into words.

Few people come to the fifth center, because they don't come even to the fourth, so how can they come to the fifth? It is very rare. Sometimes a Christ, a Buddha, or a Saraha, comes to the fifth. The beauty of even their words is tremendous—what to say about their silence? Even their words carry silence. They speak and yet they speak not. They say and they say the unsayable, the ineffable, the inexpressible.

You also use the throat, but that is not visuddhi. When that chakra truly starts functioning, your words have honey in them. Then your words have a fragrance, a music to them, a dance. Then whatever you say is poetry, whatever you utter is sheer joy.

The sixth chakra is *ajna*, which means "order." With the sixth chakra, never before it, you are in order. With the sixth chakra, never before it, you become the master. Before it you were a slave. With the sixth chakra, whatsoever you say will happen and whatsoever you desire will happen. With the sixth chakra, never before it, you have will. Before it, will does not exist.

But there is a paradox in it. With the fourth chakra, ego disappears. With the fifth chakra, all impurities disappear and then you have will—

so you cannot do harm through your will. In fact, it is no longer your will: it is the will of existence, because the ego disappears at the fourth and all impurities disappear at the fifth. Now you are the purest being, just a vehicle, an instrument, a messenger. Now you have will because you are not—now the will of existence is your will.

Very rarely does a person come to this sixth chakra because this is the last, in a way. In the world, this is the last. Beyond this is the seventh, but then you enter a totally different world, a separate reality. The sixth is the last boundary line, the last outpost.

The seventh is *sahasrar*, which means "one-thousand-petaled lotus." When your energy moves to the seventh, sahasrar, you become a lotus. Now you need not go to any other flower for honey—now the bees start coming to you. Now you attract bees from the whole earth. Your sahasrar has opened and your lotus is in full bloom. This lotus is Nirvana.

The lowest is muladhar. From the lowest, life is born—the life of the body and the senses. With the seventh, again life is born—life eternal, not of the body, not of the senses.

This is the Tantra physiology. It is not the physiology of the medical books. Please don't look for it in the medical books—it is not there. It is a metaphor, it is a way of speaking. It is a map to make things understandable. If you move in this way, you will never come to that cloudiness of thoughts. If you avoid the fourth chakra, then you go into the head. To be in the head means not to be in love; to be in thoughts means not to be in trust; to be thinking means not to be looking.

tantra is transcendence

Tantra is transcendence. It is neither indulgence nor repression. It is walking on a tightrope in one of the greatest of balances. It is not as easy as it appears—it needs delicate awareness. It is a great harmony.

It is easy for the mind to indulge. The opposite is also easy, to renounce. To move to the extreme is easy for the mind. To remain in the middle, exactly in the middle, is the most difficult thing for the mind because it is a suicide for the mind. The mind dies in the middle and the no-mind arises. That's why Buddha has called his path *majjhim nikaya*—the middle path.

Saraha is a disciple of Buddha—in the same lineage, with the same understanding, with the same awareness. This fundamental point has to be understood; otherwise, you will misunderstand Tantra. What is this razor's edge? What is this being exactly in the middle?

To indulge in the world, no awareness is needed. To repress worldly desires, no awareness is needed. Your so-called worldly people and your otherworldly people are not very different. They may be standing back-to-back, but they are of exactly the same type of mind. Somebody is hankering for money, and somebody is so against money that he is afraid even to look at currency. These people are not different—for both of them, money is of great importance. One is in greed and one is in fear, but the importance of the money is the same—both are obsessed with money.

One is continuously thinking of women, dreaming, fantasizing, while another has become so afraid that he has escaped to the Himalayas to avoid women—but both are the same. For both, the woman is important, or the man; *the other* is important. One seeks the other, one avoids the other, but the other remains their focus.

Tantra says: The other has not to be the focus, neither this way nor that way. This can happen only through great understanding. The lust for another has to be understood—neither indulged in nor avoided, but understood.

Tantra is scientific. The word *science* means understanding. The word *science* means knowing. Tantra says: Knowing liberates. If you know exactly what greed is, you are free of greed and there is no need to renounce it. The need to renounce arises only because you have not understood what greed is. The need to take a vow against sex is needed only because you have not understood what sex is.

And society does not allow you to understand it. Society helps you *not* to understand. Society has been avoiding the subjects of sex and death down through the centuries. These subjects are not to be thought about, not to be contemplated, not to be discussed, written about, or researched; they are to be avoided. Through that avoidance, a great ignorance has existed about them and that ignorance is the root cause. There are two types of people who act out of that ignorance: one who indulges madly and one who becomes tired and escapes.

Tantra says: The one who is indulging madly will never understand, because he will simply be repeating a habit. He will never look into the habit or the root cause of it, and the more he indulges the more mechanical he becomes.

Have you not observed it? Your first love had something superb, the second was not so superb, the third was even more ordinary, and the fourth, mundane. What happened? Why has the first love been so praised? Why have people always said that love happens only once? Because the first time it was not mechanical, so you were a little more alert about it. The next time, you were expecting it: you were not so alert. The third time, you thought you knew about it, so there was no exploration in it. The fourth time it was mundane; you settled into a mechanical habit.

Through indulgence, sex becomes a habit. Yes, it gives a little release, just like a sneeze— but not more than that. It is a physical release of energy. You become too burdened with energy and you have to throw out that energy just to gather it again through food, through exercise, through sunlight. Again gather it and again throw it out. That's what the person who indulges goes on doing: he creates great energy and then throws it out for no purpose, with no significance. Having it, he suffers the tension of it. Throwing it out, he suffers the weakness of it. He simply suffers.

Never think that the one who indulges is happy. Never! He is the most miserable person in the world. How can he be happy? He hopes, he desires happiness, but he never achieves it.

Remember that in saying these things, Tantra does not propose that you move to the other extreme.

Tantra is not saying that you should escape from this world of indulgence. Escaping will again become a mechanical habit. While the man is sitting in a cave, the woman will not be available, but that doesn't make much difference. If at any time the woman does become available, the man who has renounced will be more prone to fall than the man who was indulging in the world. Whatever you repress becomes powerful within you. Whatever you repress will become your attraction and will have a magnetic pull on you. The repressed becomes powerful; it gains power out of all proportion.

Listen to this anecdote:

Deep in a beautiful woodland park stood two lovely bronze statues: a boy and a girl, posed in attitudes of love and longing. They had stood thus for three hundred years, their arms held out yearningly to each other, yet never touching. One day a magician passed by and with compassion said, "I have enough power to give them life for one hour, so I am going to do this. For one hour they will be able to kiss, to touch, to embrace, to make love to each other." So the magician waved his magic wand. Immediately the statues leaped off their pedestals, and hand in hand ran into the shrubbery.

There was a great commotion, loud thumps, shouts, squawkings and flutterings. With irresistible curiosity, the magician tiptoed over and peered into the leaves.

The boy was holding down a bird, over which the girl squatted. Suddenly he jumped up. "Now it is your turn to hold him down while I shit on him!" he exclaimed.

Three hundred years of birds shitting on them... then who bothers about lovemaking? That was their repression.

You can sit in a cave and become a statue, but that which you have repressed will hover around you. It will be the only thing that you will ever think about. Tantra says: Beware. Beware of indulgence and beware of renunciation. Beware of both—both are traps. Either way, you are trapped in the mind.

Then where is the way?

Tantra says: Awareness is the way. Indulgence is mechanical, repression is mechanical; both are mechanical things. The only way out of mechanical things is to become aware, alert. Don't go to the Himalayas, bring about a Himalayan silence within you. Don't escape, become more awake. Look into things deeply with no fear... without fear, look into things deeply. Don't listen to what your so-called religious people are teaching. They make you afraid; they don't allow you to look into sex, they don't allow you to look into death. They have exploited your fears tremendously.

The only way for someone to exploit you is to first make you afraid. Once you are afraid, you are ready to be exploited. Fear is the basis and has to be created first. You have been made afraid. Sex is sin, so is fear. Even while making love to your woman or man, you never look directly into it. Even while making love, you are avoiding it. You are making love and avoiding sex. You don't want to see into the reality of it—what it is exactly, why it infatuates you, why it has a magnetic pull over you. Why? What is it exactly, how does it arise, how does it take possession of you, what does it give you, and where does it lead? What happens in it and what happens out of it? Where do you arrive again and again making love? Do you arrive anywhere? These things have to be encountered.

Tantra is an encounter with the reality of life. Sex is fundamental. So is death. They are the two most basic, fundamental chakras— muladhar and svadisthan. When you understand them, the third chakra opens. When you understand the third, the fourth opens, and so on and so forth. When you have understood the six chakras, that understanding hits the seventh chakra and it blooms into a one-thousand-petaled lotus. That day is of superb glory. That day is the meeting day, the day of cosmic orgasm. That day you embrace the divine and the divine embraces you. That day the river disappears into the ocean forever and ever. Then there is no coming back.

From each state of your mind, understanding has to be gained. Wherever you are, don't be afraid. That is the Tantra message: Wherever you are, don't be afraid. Drop only one thing— fear. Only one thing has to be feared, and that is fear. Unafraid, with great courage, look into the reality, whatever the reality is. If you are a thief, then look into that. If you are an angry person, look into that. If you are greedy, look into that. Wherever you are, look into it. Don't escape. Looking into it, go through it. Watching, go

through it. If you can walk the path into greed, into sex, into anger, into jealousy, with eyes open, you will be freed of it.

This is the Tantra promise: Truth liberates. Knowing frees. Knowing is freedom. Otherwise, whether you repress or you indulge, the end is the same.

It happened:

There was a man who had a most attractive wife. But he began to be suspicious of her. At last he could stand it no longer. Being on the night shift, he asked the foreman for a pass out, and went home at two in the morning to find his best friend's car outside, just as he had feared. He let himself in, crept up the stairs and rushed into his wife's bedroom. There she lay on top of the bed, stark naked, but smoking a cigarette and reading a book.

He went wild and searched under the bed and in the closet but he could not find any man. He went berserk and wrecked the bedroom. Then he started on the living room—he threw the TV out of the window, slashed the armchairs, overturned the table and sideboard. Then he turned his attention to the kitchen, where he smashed all the dishes and then he threw the fridge out of the window. Then he shot himself.

When he got up to heaven's gates, who should he see waiting for admission but his late best friend, who asked him, "What are you doing up here?"

The wronged husband explained all about how he had lost his temper, and added, "But how does it come about that you are up here, too?"

"Ah, me? I was in the fridge."

Both end the same way—whether you are in the Himalayan cave or in the world does not make much difference. The life of indulgence and the life of repression both end in the same way because their mechanism is no different. Their appearance is different, but their inner quality is the same.

Awareness brings a different quality to your life. With awareness, things start changing, changing tremendously—not that you change them, no, not at all. A person of awareness does not change anything, and a person of

unawareness continuously tries to change everything. But the person of unawareness never succeeds in changing anything and the person of awareness simply finds change happening, tremendous change happening.

It is awareness that brings change, not your effort. Why does it happen through awareness? Because the awareness changes *you*, and when you are different the whole world is different. It is not a question of creating a different world, it is only a question of creating a different *you*. You are your world, so if you change, the world

> ❝ *You are your world, so if you change, the world changes.* ❞

changes. If you don't change, you can go on changing the whole world but nothing changes; you will create the same world again and again.

You create your world. It is out of you that your world is projected. Tantra says: Awareness is the key, the master key that opens all the doors of life.

Remember, it is delicate. If I talk about the foolishness of repression, you start thinking about indulging. If I talk about the foolishness of indulgence, you start thinking about repression. It happens every day: you move to the opposite immediately. But the whole point is not to be tempted by the opposite.

To be tempted by the opposite is to be tempted by the Devil. That is the Devil in the Tantra system: to be tempted by the opposite. There is no other devil. The only Devil is that the mind can play a trick on you: it can propose the opposite. You are against indulgence? The mind says, "So simple… now repress. Don't indulge, escape. Drop this whole world. Forget all about it." But how can you forget all about it? Is it so simple to forget all about it? Then why are you escaping far away and why are you afraid? If you can forget all about it so simply, then be here and forget all about it. But you can't be here. You know the world will tempt you. This momentary understanding, this false

understanding that you think you have, will not be of much use. When the temptation comes from desires, you will be a victim. You know it. Before it happens you want to escape, you want to escape fast. You want to escape from the opportunity. Why? Why do you want to escape from the opportunity?

In India, the so-called saints won't stay with householders. Why? What is the fear? In India, the so-called saints won't touch a woman, won't even look. Why? What is the fear? From where does this fear come? They are just avoiding the opportunity. But to avoid the opportunity is not a great achievement.

Just avoiding the opportunity is not of much use. It is a false facade. You can believe in it, but you cannot deceive existence. In fact, you cannot even deceive yourself. In your dreams, that which you have left behind in a repressive way will pop up again and again. It will drive you crazy. Your so-called saints are not even able to sleep well; they are afraid of sleep. Why? Because in sleep, the world that they have repressed asserts itself in dreams; the unconscious starts relating its desires. The unconscious says, "What are you doing here? You are a fool." The unconscious spreads its net again.

While you are awake you can repress, but when you are asleep, how can you repress? You lose all control. The conscious mind represses, but the conscious mind goes to sleep. That's why in all the old traditions saints have always been afraid of sleep. They cut down their sleep from eight hours to seven, from seven to six, from six to five… four, three, two. And foolish people think it a great achievement. They think, "This saint is a great saint. He sleeps only two

hours." In fact, he is simply showing one thing: that he is afraid of his unconscious. He does not allow the unconscious time to surface.

When you sleep for two hours, the unconscious cannot surface, because those two hours are needed for the body's rest. You dream better dreams—good dreams, beautiful dreams—during the time after your sleep is complete. That's why you dream better in the morning, in the early morning. First the need of the body has to be taken care of; the body needs rest. Once the body has rested, then the mind needs rest—that is a secondary thing.

And when the mind takes its rest, then the unconscious, in a restful mood, releases its desires and dreams arise.

The second thing is that if you only rest for two hours in the night there may be dreams, but you will not be able to remember them. That's why you remember only the late dreams, those that you dream early in the morning. You forget the other dreams of the night because you are so deeply asleep that you cannot remember them. So the saint thinks he has not dreamed about sex, he has not dreamed about money, he has not dreamed about power, prestige, respectability. If he sleeps for two hours, the sleep is so deep and

it is such a necessity for the body that it is almost like a coma, so he cannot remember.

You remember dreams only when you are half awake and half asleep. Then the dream can be remembered, because it is close to the conscious. Half asleep, half awake, something of the dream filters into your consciousness, moves into the conscious mind. In the morning you can remember a little bit of it.

That's why you will be surprised that if you ask a laborer who works hard the whole day, "Do you dream?" he will say, "No." Everybody dreams, but not everybody can remember. Working hard the whole day, eight hours, chopping wood or digging a ditch or breaking stones is such hard work that when you fall asleep you are almost in a coma. Dreams come, but you cannot remember them, you cannot recapture them.

So listen to your body, your bodily needs. Listen to your mind, listen to your mind's needs. Don't avoid them. Go into those needs, explore them with loving care. Befriend your body, befriend your mind, if you want to get beyond them one day. Befriending is essential.

That is the Tantra vision of life: Befriend your life energies. Don't become antagonistic.

the four mudras

Tantra describes four seals, or **mudras**. *To attain the ultimate, a person passes through four doors and has to open four locks. Those four locks are called the four seals, or four* **mudras**. *These are very important.*

The first mudra is called Karma Mudra. It is the outermost door, the very periphery of your being. It is the outermost area—just like action, that's why it is called Karma Mudra. *Karma* means "action." Action is the outermost core of your being; it is your periphery. What you *do* is your periphery. You love somebody, you hate somebody, you kill somebody, you protect somebody—what you do is your periphery. Action is the outermost part of your being.

The first seal is opened by becoming total in your action… *total* in your action. Whatever you do, do totally, and there will arise great joy. If you are angry, be totally angry; you will learn much from total anger. If you are totally angry and fully aware of your anger, anger will disappear one day. There will be no point in being angry anymore. Once you have understood it, it can be dropped.

Anything that is understood can be dropped easily. Only things not understood continue hanging around you. Try to be total and alert—this is the first lock to be opened.

Remember always, Tantra is scientific. It does not tell you to repeat a mantra. It says, Become aware in your action.

The second seal is called Gyana Mudra—a little deeper than the first, a little more inward than the first—like knowledge. *Gyana* means "knowledge." Action is the outermost thing and knowledge is a little deeper. You can watch what I am doing, but you cannot watch what I am knowing. Knowing is internal. Actions can be watched; knowings cannot be watched. The second seal is that of knowing, Gyana Mudra.

Now, start knowing what you really know, and stop believing things that you really don't know. Somebody asks you, "Is there a God?" and you say, "Yes, God exists"—remember, do you really know? If you don't, please don't say you do. Say, "I don't know." If you are honest and only say what you know, and only believe what you know, the second seal will be broken. If you go on believing things that you don't really know, the second seal will never be broken. False knowledge is the enemy of true knowledge. All beliefs are false knowledge; you simply believe them. Your so-called saints keep telling you, "First believe, then you will know."

Tantra says, First *know*, then belief is there. But that is a totally different kind of belief—it is trust. You "believe in" God; you *know* the sun. The sun rises; you need not believe in it—it is

simply there and you *know* it. God you "believe in." That God is bogus.

There is another God—the godliness that comes through knowing. But the first thing is to drop all that you don't know but only *believe* that you know. You have always believed and you have always carried the load—drop that load. Out of a hundred things you will be unburdened of almost ninety-eight—unburdened.

Only a few things will remain that you truly *know*. You will feel great freedom. Your head will not be so heavy. With that freedom and weightlessness, you enter the second mudra. The second seal is broken.

The third mudra is called Samaya Mudra. *Samaya* means "time." The first outermost layer is action, the second layer is knowing, the third layer is time. Knowledge has disappeared and you are only in the now; only the purest of time remains.

Meditate over it. In the *now*, there is no knowledge. Knowledge is always about the past. In the now-moment there is no knowledge; it is completely free from knowledge. Just this moment, what do you know? Nothing is known. If you start thinking that you know this and that,

it will come from the past. It will not come from *this* moment, not from *now*. Knowledge is either from the past or it is a projection into the future. The *now* is pure of knowledge.

So the third is Samaya Mudra—to be in this moment. Why does Tantra call it *samaya*, time? Ordinarily you think that past, present, and future are three divisions of time, but that is not the Tantra understanding. Tantra says: Only the present is time. The past is not, it has already gone. The future is not, it has not yet come. Only the present is.

To be in the present is to be truly in time. Otherwise, you are either in memory or you are in dreams, which are both false, delusions. So the third seal is broken by being in the now.

First, be total in your action and the first seal is broken. Second, be honest in your knowing and the second seal is broken. Now, be just here and now and the third seal is broken.

The fourth seal is called *mahamudra*, "the great gesture." It is the innermost layer, like space. Now, only purest space remains. Action, knowing, time, space—these are the four seals. Space is your innermost core, the hub of the wheel, or the center of the cyclone.

In your innermost emptiness is space, sky.

PLEASURE, JOY, BLISS

The first pleasure is when your energy is flowing out—bodily pleasure. Joy is when your energy is flowing in—subjective, psychological joy. And when does bliss happen? When your energy is not flowing anywhere—when it is simply there. You are not going anywhere, you are simply there: you are just a being. Now you don't have any goals and you don't have any desires to fulfill. You don't have a future; you are just here now. When the energy has become just a pool—not going anywhere, not flowing anywhere, no goal to be attained, nothing to be sought, you are just here, tremendously here, totally here; this *now* is all the time that is left for you, and this *here* is all the space—then suddenly this gathering of energy that is not moving anywhere and is not distracted by body or mind, becomes a great rush in you. And the one-thousand-petaled lotus opens. So, joy and pleasure are the buds, grace and gratitude and glory are the leaves, and this ultimate flowering of bliss is the fulfillment, the fruition. You have come home.

essentials of the
tantra vision

Real Tantra is not technique but love. It is not technique but prayerfulness. It is not head-oriented but a relaxation into the heart. Please remember it. Many books have been written on Tantra, and they all talk about technique. But the real Tantra has nothing to do with technique. The real Tantra cannot be written about; the real Tantra has to be imbibed.

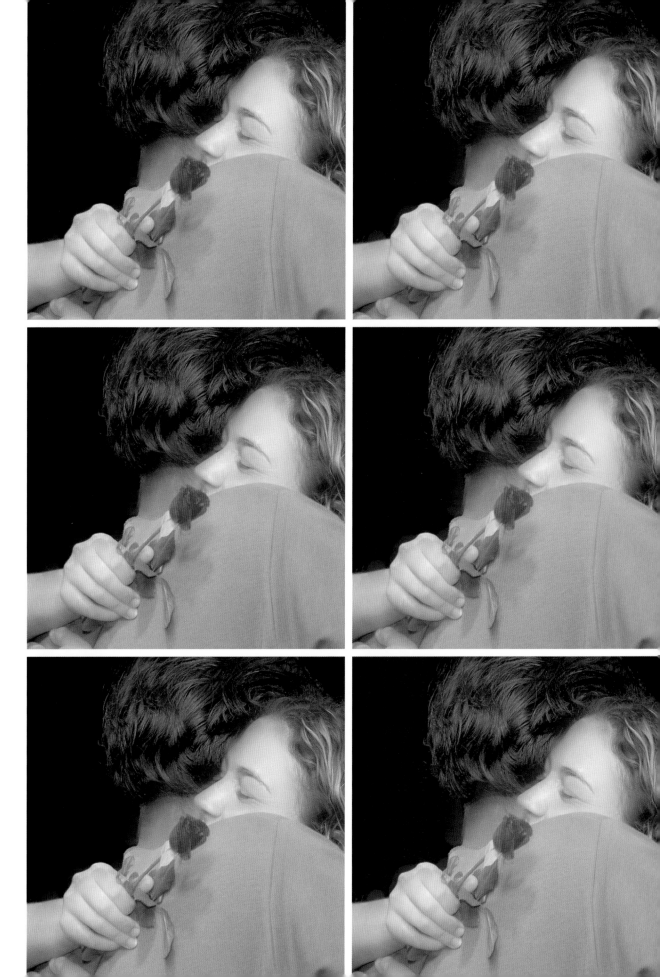

the way of intelligence

There are two ways to approach reality: the way of the intellect and the way of intelligence.

The way of the intellect is to theorize, to think about, to speculate. All speculation is meaningless,

because how can you speculate about that which you don't know? How can you even think about

that which you don't know?

The unknown cannot be thought—there is no way to think about the unknown. All that you think is the known that goes on repeating in your mind. Yes, you can create new combinations of old thoughts, but just by making new combinations, you are not going to discover the real. You will be deceiving yourself.

Intellect is the greatest deceiver in the world. Through intellect man has deceived himself down the ages. Through intellect you *explain away* the reality, you don't explain it. Through intellect you create such a dust around yourself that you cannot see the reality at all, and you are cut off from the existential. You are lost in your scriptures—no one has ever been lost anywhere else. It is in the jungle of the scriptures where you get lost.

Tantra is the way of intelligence, not of intellect. It does not answer any questions, it does not explain anything at all; it is non-explanatory. It is not a questioning, it is a quest. It is not inquiry *about* the truth, it is an inquiry *into* the truth. It penetrates reality. It tries to destroy all the clouds that surround you so that you can see the reality as it is.

Tantra is to go beyond thinking. That's why love has been so much praised by the tantrikas. That's why the orgasm has become a symbol for the ultimate reality. The reason is that it is only in orgasm that you lose your mind for a few moments. That is the only state of no-mind that is available to the ordinary person. That is the only possibility for you to have a glimpse of reality.

Hence, sexual orgasm has become tremendously important on the path of Tantra. Not because it gives you ultimate reality, but because at least it gives you a chance to peek beyond the mind. It gives you a small window—momentary—it does not stay long, but still it is the only possibility for you to have some contact with reality. Otherwise, you are always surrounded by your thoughts and your thoughts explain nothing. All explanations are simply nonsense.

To know the truth, you are moving into the greatest adventure there is. You may be lost, who knows?

The reality of a human being is a mystery. There is no answer that can answer it, because it is not a question in the first place. It is a mystery to be lived, not a problem to be solved. Remember the distinction between a problem and a mystery: a mystery is existential, a problem is intellectual. The mystery is not created by the mind, so the mind cannot solve it. The problem is created by the mind in the first place so the mind can solve it. But the mystery of life—this existential mystery that surrounds you, these trees, these stars, these birds, people, you yourself—how can you explain them through the mind?

The mind is a recent arrival. Existence has lived without the mind for a long time. The mind is a recent addition that has just happened. Scientists say that if we divide human history into twenty-four hours, into one day, then the mind came just a few seconds ago... just seconds ago! How can it solve anything? What can it solve? It has not known the beginning, it has not known the end; it has come just now in the middle. It has no perspective.

If you want to know what this unknown is, you have to drop out of the mind, you have to disappear into existence. That is the Tantra way.

Tantra is not a philosophy. Tantra is absolutely existential. And remember, when I say that Tantra is existential, I don't mean the existentialism of Sartre, Camus, Marcel, and others. That existentialism is a philosophy, a philosophy of existence, but not the Tantra way. And the difference is vast.

The existential philosophers in the West have only stumbled upon the negative: anguish, angst, depression, sadness, anxiety, hopelessness, meaninglessness, purposelessness—all the negatives. Tantra has stumbled upon all that is beautiful, joyful, blissful. Tantra says: Existence is an orgasm, an eternal orgasm going on and on and on. It is forever and ever an orgasm, an ecstasy.

They must be moving in different directions. Sartre thinks about existence. Tantra says, Thinking is not the door; it leads nowhere. It is a blind alley. It brings you only to a cul-de-sac. Philosophy is great if you are just fooling around. Then philosophy is great: you can make mountains out of molehills and you can enjoy the trip.

Philosophy is creating mountains out of molehills. You can go on and on—there is no end to it. For at least five thousand years, people have been philosophizing about each and every thing: about the beginning, about the end, about the middle. Yet not a single question has been solved. Not a single—not the smallest—question has been solved or dissolved. Philosophy has proved to be the most futile of efforts. But still we continue, knowing perfectly well that it never delivers anything. Why? It promises, but it never delivers. Then why do we continue with this effort?

Philosophy is cheap. It does not require any involvement; it is not a commitment. You can sit in your chair and think. It is a dream. It does not require you to change in order to see reality. That's where courage is needed; adventurous courage is needed.

To know the truth, you are moving into the greatest adventure there is. You may be lost, who knows? You may never come back, who knows? Or you may come back utterly changed, and who knows whether it will be for the good or not?

The journey is unknown, so unknown that you cannot even plan it. You have to take a jump into it. Blindfolded, you have to jump into it, in the dark night, with no map, not knowing where you are going, not knowing what you are going for. Only a few daredevils enter into this existential quest. Tantra has only appealed to a few people, but those were the salt of the earth.

beyond indulgence

Tantra is not a way of indulgence. It is the only way to get out of indulgence. It is the only way to get out of sexuality. No other way has ever been helpful for humanity; all other ways have made people more and more sexual.

Sex has not disappeared—the moralists have only poisoned it more and more. It is still there in a poisoned form. Yes, guilt has arisen in human beings, but sex has not disappeared. It cannot disappear because it is a biological reality. It is existential; it cannot simply be made to disappear by repressing it. It can disappear only when you become so aligned that you can release the energy encapsulated in sexuality—the energy is released not by repression but by understanding. Once the energy is released, out of the mud comes the lotus. The lotus has to come up out of the mud; it has to go higher. Repression takes it deeper into the mud.

The whole of humanity has repressed sex in the mud of the unconscious. People go on repressing it, sitting on top of it; not allowing it to move. They kill it by fasting, by discipline, by going to a cave in the Himalayas, by moving to a monastery where women are not allowed. There are monasteries where no woman has ever entered for hundreds of years; there are convents where only nuns have lived and a man has never entered. These are ways of repressing and they create more and more sexuality and more and more dreams of indulgence.

No, Tantra is not a way of indulgence. It is the only way of freedom. Tantra says: Whatever exists has to be understood, and through understanding, changes occur of their own accord.

Indulgence is suicidal—as suicidal as repression. These are the two extremes that Buddha says to avoid. One extreme is repression, the other is indulgence. Be in the middle: neither be repressive nor indulgent. Just be in the middle, watchful, alert, aware. It is your life! Neither does it have to be repressed, nor does it have to be wasted—it has to be understood.

It is your life—take care of it, love it, befriend it! If you can befriend your life, it will reveal many mysteries to you, it will take you to the very door of the beyond.

Tantra is not indulgence at all. Repressive people have always thought that Tantra is indulgence because their minds are so much obsessed. For example, how can a man who lives in a monastery without ever seeing a woman believe that Saraha

is not indulging when he lives with a woman? Not only lives with a woman but practices strange things: sitting with the woman naked while he just watches her; or even while making love to the woman, he watches himself and his lovemaking.

Now, you cannot see his watching; you can see only that he is making love to a woman. And if you are repressive, your whole repressed sexuality will bubble up. You will start going mad! You will project all that you have repressed in yourself onto Saraha—and Saraha is not doing anything like that; he is moving in a totally different dimension. He is not really interested in the body. He wants to see what this sexuality is; he wants to see what this appeal of sex is; he wants to see what exactly orgasm is; he wants to be meditative in that peak moment so that he

can find the clue and the key… maybe there is the key to open the door of the beyond. In fact, it is there.

Nature has hidden the key in your sexuality. On the one hand, through your sexuality, life survives but that is only a partial use of your sex energy. On the other hand, if you move with full awareness into your sex energy, you will find a key that can help you enter the eternal. One small aspect of sex is that your children will be born. The other aspect, a higher aspect, is that you can live in eternity.

Sex energy is life energy. Ordinarily we don't move further than the porch. We never go into the palace. Saraha is trying to go into the palace. The people who came to the king must have been suppressed people—as all people are suppressed.

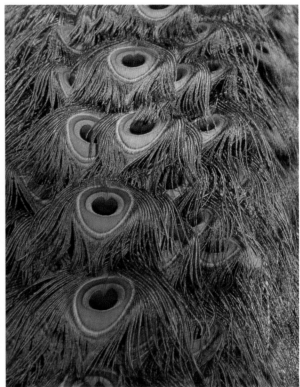

The politician and the priest have to teach suppression because it is only through suppression that people can be driven insane. You can rule insane people more easily than sane people. And when people are insane in their sex energy, they start moving in other directions—they start moving toward money or power or prestige. They have to express their sex energy somewhere or other; it is boiling and they have to release it. So money-madness or power-addiction becomes their release.

This whole society is sex-obsessed. If sex-obsession disappears from the world, people will not be money-mad. Who will bother about money? And people will not be bothered by power. Nobody will want to become a president or a prime minister—for what? Life is so tremendously beautiful in its ordinariness, it is so superb in its ordinariness, why should anyone want to become "somebody"? Being nobody is so delicious—nothing is missing. But if you destroy people's sexuality and repress them, so much is missing that they are always hankering, thinking that somewhere there must be joy, because here it is missing.

Sex is one of the activities given by nature in which you are thrown again and again to the present moment. Ordinarily you are never in the present, except when you are making love, and then too for only a few seconds.

Tantra says you have to understand sex, to decode sex. If sex is so vital that life comes out of it, then there must be something more to it. That something more is the key to transcendence.

beyond the taboo

Why has sex been a taboo in all societies down the ages? It is a complicated question, but important too—worth going into.

Sex is the most powerful human instinct. The politician and the priest have understood from the very beginning that sex is the most driving human energy. It has to be curtailed; it has to be cut. If people are allowed total freedom in sex, then there will be no possibility of dominating them; making slaves out of them will be impossible.

Have you not seen it being done? When you want a bull to be yoked to a cart, what do you do? You castrate him—you destroy his sex energy. And have you seen the difference between a bull and an ox? What a difference! An ox is a poor phenomenon, a slave. A bull is a beauty; a bull is a glorious phenomenon, a great splendor. See a bull walking, how he walks like an emperor! Then see an ox pulling a cart.

The same has been done to human beings: the sex instinct has been curtailed, cut, crippled. A man does not exist as a bull now, he exists like the ox, and each man is pulling a thousand and one carts. Look, and you will find behind you a thousand and one carts, and you are yoked to them all.

Why can't you yoke a bull? The bull is too powerful. If he sees a cow passing by, he will throw aside both you and the cart and he will go to the cow. He will not bother a bit about who

you are and he will not listen to you. It will be impossible to control the bull.

Sex energy is life energy; it is uncontrollable. The politician and the priest are not interested in you, they are interested in channeling your energy in other directions. So there is a certain mechanism behind it that has to be understood.

Sex repression, tabooing sex, is the very foundation of human slavery. People cannot be free unless sex is free. People cannot be truly free unless their sex energy is allowed natural growth.

These are the five tricks through which the human being has been turned into a slave, an ugly phenomenon, a cripple.

The first: Keep people as weak as possible if you want to dominate them. If the priest wants to dominate you or the politician wants to dominate you, you must be kept as weak as possible. Yes, in certain cases, exceptions are allowed—that is, when the service of fighting the enemy is needed. The army is allowed many things that other people are not allowed. The army is in the service of death; it is allowed to be powerful. It is allowed to remain as powerful as possible because it is needed to kill the enemy.

Other people are destroyed. They are forced to remain weak in a thousand and one ways, and the best way to keep a person weak is not to give love total freedom. Love is nourishment. Psychologists have discovered that if a child is not given love, he shrivels up into himself and becomes weak. You can give him milk, you can give him medicine, you can give him everything else, just don't give love. Don't hug him, don't kiss him, don't hold him close to the warmth of your body and the child will become weaker and weaker. There are more chances of his dying than surviving. What happens? Why? Just hugging, kissing, giving warmth, somehow the child feels nourished, accepted, loved, needed. The child starts feeling worthy; the child starts feeling a certain meaning in his life. From childhood we starve children: we don't give love as much as is needed. Then we force the young men and young women not to fall in love unless they get married. By the age of fourteen, they become sexually mature. But their education may take more time—ten years more, twenty-four, twenty-five years—then they will be getting their MAs, or PhDs, or MDs, so we have to force them not to fall in love.

Sexual energy comes to its climax near the age of eighteen. Never again will a man be so potent and never again will a woman be able to have a greater orgasm than she can experience near the age of eighteen. But we try to force them not to make love. We force boys and girls to have separate dormitories. Girls and boys are kept separate, and between the two stands the whole mechanism of police, magistrates, chancellors, principals, headmasters. They are all holding the boys back from going to the girls, holding the girls back from going to the boys. Why is so much care taken? They are trying to kill the bull and create an ox.

By the time you are eighteen you are at the peak of your sexual energy, your love energy. By the time you get married you are twenty-five, twenty-six, twenty-seven... and the age has been going up and up. The more cultured a country, the longer you wait, because there is more to be learned, a job has to be found, this and that. By the time you get married you are almost declining in your powers.

Then you make love, but the lovemaking never becomes really hot—it never comes to the point where people evaporate—it remains lukewarm. And when you have not been able to love totally, you cannot love your children because you don't know how. When you have not known the peaks of love, how can you teach your children? How can you help your children to know the peaks of it?

Down the ages we have been denied love so that we should remain weak.

Second: Keep people as ignorant and deluded as possible so that they can easily be deceived. If you want to create a sort of idiocy—which is a must for the priest and the politician and their conspiracy—then the best thing is to prevent people from moving into love freely. Without love, a person's intelligence falls low. Have you not seen it? When you fall in love, suddenly all your capacities are at their peak, at their crescendo. Just a moment ago you were looking dull, and then you met your woman... and suddenly a great joy erupted in your being; you are aflame. When people are in love, they perform at their maximum. When love disappears or when love is not there, they perform at their minimum.

The greatest, most intelligent people are the most sexual people. This has to be understood, because love energy is basically intelligence. If you cannot love, you are closed and cold; you cannot flow. While in love you flow. While in love, you feel so confident that you can touch the stars. That's why a woman becomes a great inspiration or a man becomes a great inspiration. When a woman is loved, she becomes more beautiful *immediately*, instantly! Just a moment ago she was an ordinary woman and now love has showered upon her—she is bathed in a totally new energy and a new aura arises around her. She walks more gracefully—a dance has entered her step. Her eyes have tremendous beauty now, her face glows, she is luminous. And the same things happen to the man.

When people are in love they perform at the optimum. Don't allow love and they will remain at the minimum. When they remain at the minimum, they are stupid, they are ignorant, they don't bother to know. When people are ignorant and stupid and deluded, they can be easily deceived. When people are sexually repressed, when their love is repressed, they start hankering for the "other life." They think about heaven or paradise, but they don't think to create the paradise here and now.

When you are in love, paradise is here and now. Then you don't bother to go to the priest. Then who worries about a paradise? You are already there! You are no longer interested. But when your love energy is repressed, you start thinking, "Here there is nothing. Now is empty. There must be somewhere, some goal...." You go to the priest and ask about heaven and he paints beautiful pictures of heaven.

Sex has been repressed so that you can become interested in the other life. And when people are interested in the other life, naturally they are not interested in this life.

Tantra says: This life is the only life. The other life is hidden in this life. It is not against it, it is not away from it; it is *in* it. Go into it. *This is it!* Go into it and you will find the other, too. God is hidden in the world—that is the Tantra message. A great message, superb, incomparable: God is hidden in the world, God is hidden here now. If you love, you will be able to feel it.

The third secret: Keep people as frightened as possible. The sure way is to not allow them

> *Tantra teaches you to reclaim respect for the body, love for the body.*

love, because love destroys fear... "Love casteth out fear." When you are in love, you are not afraid. When you are in love, you can fight against the whole world. When you are in love, you feel infinitely capable of anything. But when you are not in love, you are afraid of small things. When you are not in love, you become more interested in security, in safety. When you are in love, you are more interested in adventure, in exploration.

People have not been allowed to love because that is the only way to make them afraid. And when they are afraid and trembling, they are always on their knees, kneeling to the priest and bowing to the politician.

It is a great conspiracy against humanity. It is a great conspiracy against you! Your politician and your priest are your enemies, but they pretend that they are public servants. They say, "We are here to serve you, to help you attain a better life. We are here to create a good life for you." Yet they are the destroyers of life itself.

The fourth: Keep people as miserable as possible—because miserable people are confused, miserable people have no self-worth, miserable people are self-condemnatory. A miserable man feels that he must have done

something wrong. A miserable woman has no grounding: you can push her from here to there—she can be turned into driftwood easily. A miserable man is always ready to be commanded, to be ordered, to be disciplined, because he knows: "On my own I am simply miserable. Maybe somebody else can discipline my life." He is a ready victim.

And the fifth: Keep people as alienated from each other as possible, so that they cannot band together for any purpose of which the priest and the politician may not approve. Keep people separate from each other. Don't allow them too much intimacy. When people are separate, lonely, and alienated from one another, they cannot band together. And there are a thousand and one tricks to keep them apart.

For example, if you are holding the hand of a man—you are a man and you are holding the hand of another man and walking down the road singing—you will feel guilty because people will start looking at you: Are you gay, homosexual or something? Two men are not allowed to be happy together. They are not allowed to hold hands, they are not allowed to hug each other. They are condemned as homosexuals. Fear arises.

If your friend comes and takes your hand in his hand, you look around: "Is somebody looking or not?" And you are in a hurry to drop his hand. You shake hands in such a hurry. Have you watched it? You just touch each other's hand and shake and you are finished. You don't hold hands; you don't hug each other. You are afraid.

Do you remember your father ever hugging you? Do you remember your mother hugging you after you became sexually mature? Why not? Fear has been created. A young man and his mother hugging? Maybe some sex will arise between them, some idea, some fantasy. Fear has been created: the father and the son, the father and the daughter, no. The brother and the sister, no; the brother and the brother—no! People are kept in separate boxes with great walls around them. Everybody is classified, and there are a thousand and one barriers.

Yes, one day, after twenty-five years of all this training, you are allowed to make love to your wife. But now the training has gone too deep into you, and suddenly you don't know

what to do. How to love? You have not learned the language. It is as if a person has not been allowed to speak for twenty-five years. For twenty-five years he has not been allowed to speak a single word and then suddenly you put him on a stage and tell him, "Give us a great lecture." What will happen? He will fall down then and there! He may faint, he may die… twenty-five years of silence, and now suddenly he is expected to deliver a great lecture? It is not possible.

This is what is happening. Twenty-five years of anti-love training, of fear, and then suddenly you are legally allowed—a license is issued—and now you can love this woman. This is your wife, you are her husband, and you are allowed to love. But what happens to those twenty-five years of wrong training? They will still be there.

Yes, you will "love"… you will make a gesture. It is not going to be explosive, it is not going to be orgasmic—it will be very tiny. That's why you are frustrated after making love. Ninety-nine percent of people are frustrated after making love, more frustrated than they have ever been before. And they think, "What is this? There is nothing in it, it is not real!" First the priest and the politician have managed things so that you have not be able to make love, and then they come and they preach that there is nothing meaningful in sex. And certainly their preaching looks right, exactly in tune with your experience. First they create the experience of futility and frustration, then they deliver their teaching. And they look logical together—of one piece.

This is a great trick, the greatest that has ever been played upon humanity. These five things can be managed through one single thing, and that is the taboo against love. It is possible to accomplish all these objectives by preventing people from loving each other. And the taboo has been managed in such a scientific way. This taboo is a great work of art—great skill and great cunningness have gone into it. It is really a masterpiece. This taboo has to be understood.

First—it is indirect. It is hidden. It is not apparent, because whenever a taboo is too obvious, it will not work. The taboo has to be hidden, so that you don't know how it works. The taboo has to be so hidden that you cannot even imagine that being against it is possible. The taboo has to go into the unconscious, not into the conscious. How to make it so subtle and so indirect?

The trick is: first go on teaching that love is great, so people never think that the priests and the politicians are against love. Go on teaching that love is great, that love is the right thing, and then don't allow any situation where love can happen. Don't allow the opportunity. Go on teaching that food is great, that eating is a great joy: "Eat as well as you can." But don't supply anything to eat. Keep people hungry and go on talking about love.

All the priests go on talking about love. Love is praised as just next to God, and every possibility of its happening is denied. Directly, they encourage it; indirectly, they cut its roots. This is the masterpiece.

No priests talk about how they have done the harm. It is as if you say to a tree, "Be green, bloom, enjoy," and then you cut the roots so that the tree cannot grow. And when the tree does not become green, you can jump upon the tree and say, "Listen! You don't listen. You don't

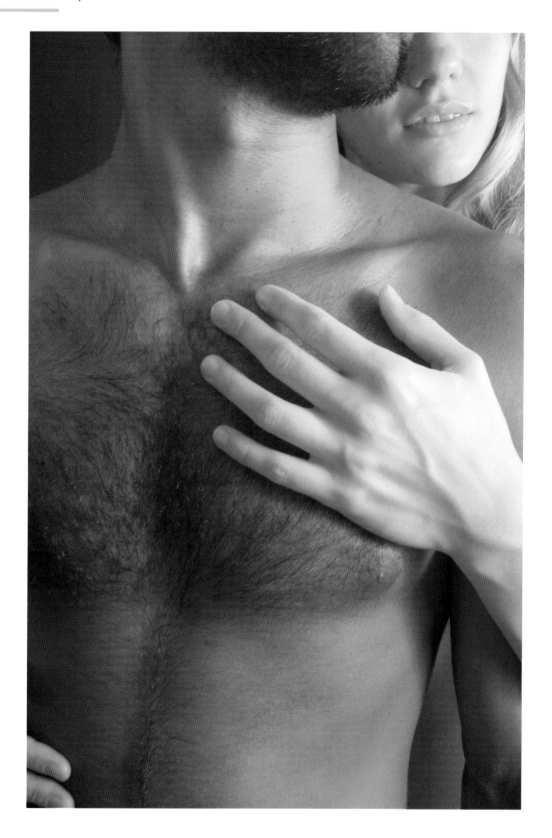

follow us. We are saying 'Be green, bloom, enjoy, dance'"... and meanwhile you go on cutting the roots.

Love is denied so much. It is the rarest thing in the world and it should not be denied. If you can love five people, you should love five. If you can love fifty, you should love fifty. If you can love five hundred, you should love five hundred. Love is so rare that the more you can spread it the better.

But you are forced into a narrow corner: you can love only your wife, you can love only your husband, you can love only this, you can love only that. It is as if there were a law that you can breathe only when you are with your wife, you can breathe only when you are with your husband. Soon breathing will become impossible. Then you will die! And you will not even be able to breathe while you are with your wife or with your husband. You have to breathe twenty-four hours a day.

Be loving.

Then there is another trick: they talk about "higher love" while they destroy the lower. They say that the lower has to be denied: bodily love is bad, spiritual love is good. Have you ever seen any spirit without a body? Have you ever seen a house without a foundation? The lower is the foundation of the higher. The body is your abode, the spirit lives in the body, with the body. You are an embodied spirit and an ensouled body. You are together. The lower and the higher are not separate, they are one—both rungs of the same ladder.

This is what Tantra wants to make clear: the lower is not to be denied, the lower has to be transformed into the higher. The lower is good.

> **The lower is not to be denied; the lower has to be transformed into the higher.**

If you are stuck with the lower, the fault is with you, not with the lower. Nothing is wrong with the lower rung of a ladder. If you are stuck with it, *you* are stuck. It is something in you.

Move.

Sex is not wrong. *You* are wrong if you are stuck there. Move higher. The higher is not against the lower; the lower makes it possible for the higher to exist.

These tricks have created many other problems. Each time you are in love, somehow you feel guilty; guilt has arisen. When there is guilt, you cannot move totally into love—the guilt prevents you, it holds you back. Even while making love to your wife or your husband, there is guilt. You know this is sin, you know you are doing something wrong. "Saints don't do it." You are a sinner. So you cannot move totally even when you are allowed—superficially—to love your spouse. The priest is hidden behind you in your guilt feelings; he is pulling you from there, pulling your strings.

When guilt arises, you start believing that you are wrong; you lose self-worth, you lose self-respect.

And another problem: When there is guilt you start pretending. Mothers and fathers don't allow their children to know that they make love: they pretend. They pretend that love does not exist. Their pretense will come to be known by the children sooner or later and when the children come to know about the pretense, they lose all trust. They feel betrayed, they feel cheated. Then fathers and mothers say that their children don't respect them. You are the cause of it—how can they respect you? You have been deceiving them in every way. You have been dishonest; you have been mean. You were telling them not to fall in love—"Beware"—and you were making love all the time. And the day will come, sooner or later, when they will realize that even their father, even their mother, was not true with them—so how can they respect you?

First guilt creates pretense, then pretense creates alienation from others. Even your own child will not feel in tune with you; there is a barrier—your pretense. And you know that everybody is pretending....

One day, you will come to know that you are just pretending and so are others. When everybody is pretending, how can you relate? When everybody is false, how can you relate? How can you be friendly when everywhere there is deception and deceit? You become disillusioned about reality, you become bitter, and you see it only as a devil's workshop. Everybody has a false face; nobody is authentic. Everybody is wearing a mask; nobody shows his original face.

You feel guilty, you feel that you are pretending, and you know that everybody is pretending, everybody is feeling guilty, and everybody has become like an ugly wound. Now it is easy to make these people slaves—to turn them into clerks, stationmasters, schoolmasters, collectors, ministers, governors, presidents. Now it is easy to distract them. You have distracted them from their roots. Sex is the root.

A curate and a bishop were in opposite corners of a railway car on a long journey. As the bishop entered, the curate put away his copy of Playboy *and started reading the* Church Times. *The bishop ignored him and began doing the* Times *crossword. Silence prevailed. After a while the curate tried to make conversation. When the bishop began to do a lot of head scratching and "tut-tut-tutting," he tried again: "Can I help you, sir?"*

"Perhaps. I am only beaten by one word. What is it that has four letters, the last three are u-n-t, and the clue is, 'essentially feminine?'"

"Why, sir," said the curate, after a slight pause. "That would be 'aunt.'"

"Of course, of course!" said the bishop. "I say, young man, can you lend me an eraser?"

When you repress things on the surface, they go deep inside, into the unconscious. It is there. Sex has not been destroyed—fortunately. It has only been poisoned. It cannot be destroyed; it is life energy. It has become polluted, and it can be purified.

Tantra can purify your sex energy. Listen to the Tantra message. Try to understand it. It is a great revolutionary message. It is against all priests and politicians. It is against all those poisoners who have killed all joy on the earth just so that people can be reduced to slaves.

Reclaim your freedom. Reclaim your freedom to love. Reclaim your freedom to be and then life will no longer be a problem. It is a mystery, it is an ecstasy, and it is a benediction.

EXPANSION

Tantra means expansion. This is the state when you have expanded to the utmost. Your boundaries and the boundaries of existence are no longer separate—they are the same. Less than that will not satisfy. When you become universal, you come home. When you become all, when you become one with all, when you are as huge as this universe, when you contain all—when stars start moving within you and earths are born in you and disappear—when you experience this cosmic expansion, then the work is finished. You have come home. This is the goal of Tantra.

without character

Be without character—that's what Tantra says. It is difficult even to understand, because down the centuries we have been taught to have character. Character means to have a rigid structure; character means the past; character means a certain enforced discipline. Character means you are no longer free—you only follow certain rules and you never go beyond those rules. You have solidity. A man of character is a solid man.

Tantra says: Drop character, be fluid, be flowing, live moment-to-moment. It does not mean irresponsibility. It means greater responsibility because it means greater awareness. When you can live through character, you need not be aware—character takes care. When you live through character, you can fall asleep easily; there is no need to be awake since the character will continue in a mechanical way. But when you don't have any character, when you don't have a hard structure around you, you have to be alert each moment. Each moment you have to see what you are doing. Each moment you have to respond to the new situation before you.

A man of character is a dead man. He has a past but no future. A man who has no character… and I am not using the word in the same sense as when you say that somebody is characterless. When you use the word "characterless" you are not using it rightly, because whomsoever you call characterless has a *character*. Maybe it is against society, but he has a character; you can depend on him, too.

The saint has a character and so does the sinner—they both have characters. You call the sinner characterless because you want to condemn his character; otherwise, he has as much character as the saint. You can depend on him: give him the opportunity and he will steal—he has character. Give him the opportunity and he is bound to steal; give him the opportunity and he will do something wrong—he has character. The moment he comes out of the jail, he starts thinking, "What to do now?" Again he is thrown in jail, again he comes out… no jail has ever cured anybody. In fact, jailing a person, imprisoning a person, makes him even cleverer, that's all. Maybe you won't be able to catch him so easily next time. But nothing else is achieved by throwing him in jail; you just give him more cleverness. He has character.

Can't you see?—a drunkard has character—a very stubborn character. A thousand and one times he vows not to drink anymore, and always his character wins over his vow and he is defeated.

The sinner has character, so has the saint.

What Tantra means by characterlessness is freedom from character. The character of the saint and the character of the sinner both make you solid like rocks, like ice. You don't have any freedom, you can't move easily. If a new situation arises you cannot respond in a new way—you have character, how can you respond in a new way? You have to respond in the old way. The old, the known, the well practiced—you are skilled in it.

A character becomes an alibi: you need not live.

Tantra says: Be characterless, be without character. Characterlessness is freedom.

A characterless person does not follow any rules—he follows his awareness. He doesn't have any discipline—he has only his consciousness. His only shelter is his consciousness. He doesn't have any conscience —his consciousness is his only shelter.

Conscience is character and it is a trick of society. Society creates a conscience in you so that you need not have any consciousness. It makes you follow certain rules for a long

> *Let life flow through you.*

time; it rewards you if you follow and it punishes you if you don't follow. It makes you a robot. Once it has created the mechanism of conscience in you, then society can be free of you—then you can be trusted, you will be a slave your whole life. It has put a conscience in you just as if Delgado had put an electrode in you; it is a subtle electrode. But it has killed you. You are no longer a flow, no longer a dynamism.

Tantra says: Walking, walk; sitting, sit; being, be! Exist without thinking. Let life flow through you without any blocks of thoughts. Let life flow through you without any fear. There is nothing to fear—you have nothing to lose. There is nothing to fear because death will take only that which birth has given to you. And it *is* going to take it anyway, so there is nothing to fear.

Let life flow through you.

s p o n t a n e i t y

In Tantra, spontaneity is the greatest value—to be natural, to allow nature to happen. Not to obstruct it, not to hinder it; not to distract it, not to take it in some direction where it was not going on its own. To surrender to nature, flow with it. Not pushing the river, but going with it all the way, wherever it leads. This trust is Tantra. Spontaneity is its mantra, its foundation.

Spontaneity means you don't interfere, you are in a let-go. Whatever happens, you watch, you are a witness to it. You know it is happening, but you don't jump into it and you don't try to change its course. Spontaneity means you don't have any direction, you don't have any goal to attain. If you have some goal to attain, you cannot be spontaneous. How can you be spontaneous if your nature is going one way, and your goal is in a different direction? How can you be spontaneous? You will drag yourself toward your goal.

That's what millions of people are doing— dragging themselves toward some imaginary goal. And because they are dragging themselves toward this goal, they are missing their natural destiny—which is the only goal! That's why there is so much frustration, so much misery, and so much hell. When you are chasing a goal, whatever you do will never satisfy your nature. That's why people seem so dull and dead. They live and yet they live not. They are moving like prisoners, chained. Their movement is not free, their movement is not a dance—it cannot be—because they are fighting constantly with themselves. There is a conflict each moment. You want to eat *this* and your religion does not approve of it; you want to go with *this* woman but that will not be respectable. You want to live *this* way, but society prohibits it. You want to be in one way, you feel that that is how you can flower, but everybody else is against it.

So do you listen to your being, or do you listen to everybody else's advice? If you listen to everybody's advice, your life will be an empty life of nothing but frustration. You will finish without ever being alive; you will die without ever knowing what life is.

But society has created such conditioning in you that it is not only outside—it is inside you. That's what conscience is all about. Whatever you want to do, your conscience says, "Don't do it!" The conscience is your parental voice; the priest and the politician speak through it. It is a great trick! They have created a conscience in you from childhood, when you were not aware at all of what was being done to you. They have put a conscience in you so that whenever you go against the conscience, you feel guilt.

Guilt means you have done something that others don't want you to do. So whenever you are natural, you feel guilty, and whenever you are not guilty, you are unnatural. This is the dilemma, this is the dichotomy, this is the problem. If you listen to your own naturalness, you feel guilty—then there is misery. You start thinking you have done something wrong. You start hiding, you start defending yourself; you start pretending that you have not done this thing. And you are afraid—somebody is bound to catch you sooner or later. You are afraid you will be caught and that brings anxiety, and guilt, and fear. You lose all love for life.

Whenever you do something against what others have taught you, you feel guilty. But whenever you do something just because others say you should, you never feel happy doing it, because it has never been your own thing to do. You are caught between these two polarities.

❝ ...you are in a let-go. ❞

I was just reading an anecdote:

"What's this double jeopardy that the Constitution is supposed to guarantee against?" Roland asked his lawyer friend, Milt.

Said Milt, "It is like this, Rollie. If you are out driving your car and both your wife and her mother are sitting in the back seat telling you how to drive, well… that's double jeopardy. And you have a constitutional right to turn around and say, 'Now, who the hell's driving this car, dear, you or your mother?'"

You may be at the wheel, but you are not driving the car. There are many people sitting in the back seat—your parents, your parents'

parents, your priest, your politician, the leader, the mahatma, the saint. They are all sitting in the back seat and they all are trying to advise you: "Do this! Don't do that! Go this way! Don't go that way!" They are driving you mad, yet you have been taught to follow them. If you don't follow them, that creates a fear in you that something is wrong—how can you be right when so many people are advising you differently? And they are always advising for your own good! How can you alone be right when the whole world is saying, "Do this!" Of course, they are in the majority and they must be right.

But remember: it is not a question of being right or wrong. It is a question of being spontaneous or not. Spontaneity is right! Otherwise, you will become an imitator, and imitators are never fulfilled human beings. You wanted to be a painter, but your parents said, "No, because painting is not going to give you enough money, and being an artist is not going to give you any respect in society. You will become a hobo, and you will be a beggar. So don't bother about painting. Become a lawyer!" So you have become a lawyer; now you don't feel any happiness. It is a plastic thing, this being a lawyer, and deep down you still want to paint.

While sitting in the court, you are still painting deep down. Maybe you are listening to the criminal, but you are thinking about his face, what a beautiful face he has and what a beautiful portrait would have been possible. You are looking at his eyes and the blueness of his eyes, and you are thinking of colors... and here you are, a prosecuting attorney! So you are constantly at unease and tension follows you.

By and by, you might start to feel that you are a respectable man—but you are just an imitation, you are artificial.

Tantra makes spontaneity the first virtue, the most fundamental virtue.

Now, one thing must be understood very deeply. Spontaneity can be of two types. One type is only impulsiveness, but then it is not very valuable. If it is of awareness, then it has a quality of being unique—the quality of a buddha. Many times you think you are becoming spontaneous when in fact you are becoming impulsive.

What is the difference between being impulsive and being spontaneous? There are two aspects to you: the body and the mind. The mind is controlled by society and the body is controlled by biology. The mind is controlled by your society because society can put thoughts into your mind; and your body is controlled by millions of years of biological evolution. The body is unconscious and so is the mind. You are a watcher, beyond both. If you stop listening to the mind and to society, there is every possibility you will start listening to your biology. Sometimes you might feel like murdering somebody, and you say, "It is good to be spontaneous, so I will do it. I have to be spontaneous." You have misunderstood. That is not going to make your life beautiful, blissful. You will be continually in conflict again—now with people outside.

By spontaneity Tantra means a spontaneity full of awareness. The first step in order to be spontaneous is to be fully aware. The moment you are aware, you are neither in the trap of the mind nor in the trap of the body. Then real

spontaneity flows from your soul—from the sky, from the sea, your spontaneity flows. Otherwise, you can change your masters: from the body you can change to the mind, or from the mind you can change to the body.

The body is fast asleep, so following the body will be like following a blind man and the spontaneity will just take you into a ditch. It is not going to help you. Impulsiveness is not spontaneity. Yes, impulse does have a certain spontaneity, more spontaneity than the mind, but it has not the quality that Tantra would like you to imbibe.

As we are now, we live unconsciously. Whether we live in the mind or in the body does not make much difference—we live unconsciously.

A drunk staggered from a tavern and started walking with one foot in the street and one on the sidewalk. After a block or two, a policeman spotted him. "Hey," said the cop. "You're drunk!"

The drunk sighed with relief. "Gosh!" he said. "Is that what's wrong? I thought I was lame."

When you are under the influence of the body, you are under the influence of chemistry. You are out of one trap, the trap of the mind, but you are in another trap, the trap of biology, chemistry. You are out of one ditch, but you have fallen into another one.

When you really want to be out of all ditches and living in freedom, you will have to become a witness of both body and mind. When you are witnessing, and your spontaneity arises out of your witnessing, that is the spontaneity Tantra is talking about.

intensity

Except for human beings, everything is fresh, because it is only we who carry the load, the luggage of memory. That's why people become dirty, unclean, loaded, burdened—otherwise, all of existence is new and fresh. It carries no past and it imagines no future. It is simply here, totally here! When you are carrying the past, much of your being is involved in the past—a past that is not. When you are imagining the future, much of your being is involved in the future, which is not, not yet. You are spread very thin; that's why your life has no intensity.

Tantra says that to know truth you need only one thing: intensity—total intensity. How to create this total intensity?

Drop the past and drop the future, then your whole life energy is focused on the small here and now. In that focusing you are afire, you are a living fire. You are the same fire that Moses saw on the mountain—and God was standing in the fire, and the fire was not burning him. The fire was not burning even the green bush; the bush was alive and fresh and young.

The whole of life is fire. To know it, you need intensity—otherwise, you live in a lukewarm way. Tantra has only one commandment: Don't live lukewarm. That is not a way to live; that is a slow suicide.

When you are eating, be intensely there. The ascetics have condemned tantrikas because they say they are just "eat, drink, and be merry" people. In a way they are right, but in another way they are wrong, because there is a great difference between the ordinary "eat, drink, and

be merry" person and a tantrika. A tantrika says this is the way to know truth—but while you are eating, then let there be *only* eating and nothing else. Then let the past disappear and the future too; then let your whole energy be poured into your food. Let there be love and affection and gratitude for the food. Chew each bite with tremendous energy and you will have not only the taste of the food but the taste of existence—because the food is part of existence! It brings life; it brings vitality. It makes you tick, it helps you stay alive. It is not just food. Food may be the container, but *life* is contained in it. If you taste only food and you don't taste existence in it, you are living a lukewarm life; then you don't know how a tantrika lives.

When you are drinking water, become thirsty! Let there be an intensity to it so that each drop of cool water gives you tremendous joy. In the very experience of those drops of water entering your throat and giving you great contentment, you will taste God—you will taste reality.

Tantra is not ordinary indulgence, it is *extraordinary* indulgence. It is not ordinary indulgence because it indulges in God himself. But, Tantra says, it is through the small things of life that you have the taste.

There are no big things in life; everything is small. The small thing becomes big and great if you enter into it utterly, totally, wholly. Making love to a woman or a man, *be* the love. Forget everything else! In that moment let there be nothing else. Let the whole existence converge on your lovemaking. Let that love be wild, innocent—innocent in the sense that there is no mind to corrupt it. Don't think about it, don't fantasize about it, because all that imagination and thinking spreads you thin. Let all thinking disappear. Let the act be total! Be in the act—lost, absorbed, gone—and then, through love, you will know what godliness is.

Tantra says it can be known through drinking, it can be known through eating, it can be known through love. It can be known from every space, from every corner, from every angle—because all angles are God's. It is all truth.

Don't think that you are unfortunate because you were not around in the beginning when God created the world—God is creating the world right now! You are fortunate to be here. You can see the creation of this moment. And don't think you will miss when the world disappears with a bang—it is disappearing right now. Each moment the world is created; each moment it disappears. Each moment it is born; each moment it dies. So Tantra says let that be your life also—each moment dying to the past; each moment being born anew.

Don't carry any load; remain empty.

While you are eating, let there be only eating and nothing else.

the unity of opposites

Those who are too analytical, interpretative, continuously thinking in categories of the mind, are always divided. They are split. There is always a problem for them. The problem is not in existence; that problem comes from their own divided minds. That person's own mind is not a single unity.

Now, you can ask the scientist, also; he says the brain is divided into two parts, the left and the right, and they function differently—not only differently, they function diametrically opposite to each other. The left side of the brain is analytical, and the right side of the brain is intuitive. The left-side mind is mathematical, logical, syllogistic. The right-side mind is poetic, artistic, esthetic, mystic. They exist according to different categories, and there is only a small bridge between the two, just a small link.

It has now and then happened that in some accident that link was broken, and the person became two. In the Second World War there were many cases where the link was broken and the man became two. Sometimes he would say one thing in the morning and by the evening he would completely forget about it and he would start saying something else. In the morning one hemisphere was working and in the evening another hemisphere was working.

Modern science has to look deeply into it. Yoga has looked deeply into it. Yoga says that

your breathing changes... for about forty minutes you breathe primarily through one nostril, and then for the next forty minutes you breathe primarily through the other nostril. Modern science has not researched why the breathing changes and what the implications of this change are. But Yoga has thought deeply about it.

When your left nostril is working, your right brain will function more; when your right nostril is working, your left brain will function more. This arrangement is so that one side of the brain can function for forty minutes and then it can rest.

Somehow, we have felt it even without knowing exactly what it is, that after each forty minutes we have to change our work. That's why in schools, colleges, and universities, they usually change the class after forty minutes. One part of the brain becomes tired. Forty minutes seems to be the ultimate limit, then it needs rest. So if you have been studying mathematics, it is good after forty minutes to study poetry; later you can come back to mathematics again.

You can watch your own life and you will find a rhythm. Just a moment ago, you were so loving toward your wife, then suddenly something clicked and you no longer feeling loving. And you are worried—what happened? Suddenly the flow is not there; you are frozen. Maybe you were holding your wife's hand and the mind changed and another mind has come in, and suddenly energy is no longer flowing. Now you want to let go of the hand and escape from this woman. Just a moment ago you were promising, "I will love you forever," and now you are worried: "This is not right. Just a moment ago I promised, and I am already breaking the promise."

You are angry and you want to hurt somebody—and just a few minutes later that anger is gone, you are no longer angry. You

> *This togetherness is the real meeting of man and woman.*

even start feeling compassion for the other person. Watch your mind and you will find this continual shift; this gear is always changing.

Tantra says there is a state of unity when the bridge between the two hemispheres of the brain is no longer a small link, but both sides are completely together. This togetherness is the real meeting of the man and the woman—because one part of the brain, the right hemisphere, is feminine while the left

hemisphere is masculine. When you are making love to a woman or a man, when orgasm happens, both hemispheres come very close. That's why the orgasm happens. It has nothing to do with the woman or the man; it has nothing to do with anything outside. It is just inside you. Watch....

Tantrikas have been watching the phenomenon of lovemaking closely, because they think, and they are right, that the greatest phenomenon on earth is love, and the greatest experience of humanity is orgasm. So if there is some truth, we must be closer to realizing that truth in the moment of orgasm than anywhere else. This is simple logic. One need not even be

> " When you feel orgasmic and happy, it has nothing to do with the other person—the whole thing is happening within you. "

logical about it; it is such an obvious thing—this is our greatest joy, so this joy must somehow be a door to the infinite. It may be slight, it may be just a part of it, but something of the infinite enters in those moments of joy. For a moment the man and woman are lost, they are no longer in their egos; their separateness disappears.

What happens exactly? You can ask physiologists, too. Tantra has discovered many things. One, when you are making love to a woman or a man and you feel orgasmic and happy, it has nothing to do with the other person—the whole thing is happening within you. It has nothing to do with the other person's orgasm; they are not related to it at all.

When the woman is having an orgasm, she is having her orgasm—it has nothing to do with the man. Maybe the man functioned as a trigger point, but the woman's orgasm is her private orgasm, and the man's orgasm is his private orgasm. You are together with the other, but your orgasm is yours; and when you are having an orgasm your partner cannot share your joy, no. It is absolutely yours. It is private. Although the other can see that something is happening

—on your face, in your body—that is just an observation from the outside. They cannot participate in it.

Even if you both have orgasms together, your orgasmic joy will not be more or less; it will not be affected by the orgasm of the other, and neither will the other's orgasm be affected by you. You are completely private, totally in yourself—that's the first thing. This means that all orgasm, deep down, is masturbatory. The woman is a help, an excuse; the man is a help, an excuse—but not a must.

The second thing that tantrikas have observed is that when the orgasm is happening, it has nothing to with your sex centers—nothing. Because if the connection from the sex center to the brain is blocked, you will have an orgasm but you will not have any joy. So, deep down, the joy of orgasm is not happening at the sex center; it is happening in the brain. Something from the sex center triggers something in the brain—it is happening in the brain. Modern research perfectly agrees with this finding of the tantrikas.

You must have heard the name of the famous psychologist, Delgado. He put electrodes in the brain and those electrodes were operated by remote control. It's possible that you could have a small remote control box, keep the box in your pocket, and any time you want to have an orgasm, you could just push a button! It would have nothing to do with your sex center; that button would just trigger something in your head—inside the head it would stimulate those centers that are stimulated by sexual energy when it is released. It would

stimulate them directly and you could have a great orgasm. Or, you could push another button and you would become immediately angry. Or you could push another button and you would fall into a deep depression. You could have all the buttons in the remote control box, and you could change your mood as you like.

When Delgado experimented with his animals for the first time, he was surprised. He fixed an electrode in his favorite mouse, which was well trained and intelligent. After Delgado fixed the electrode in the mouse's head, he gave a box to the mouse and trained him to push the button. Once the mouse knew that when the button was pushed he would have a sexual orgasm, he went mad. In one day, he pressed the button hundreds and hundreds of times. He died because he would not do anything else. He would not eat or sleep, he forgot everything else. He just went crazy pushing the button again and again.

This modern research into the human brain says exactly what Tantra has been saying. First, the orgasm has nothing to do with the person outside—your woman or your man.

Second, it has nothing to do with your sex energy. The other person triggers your sex energy, your sex energy triggers your brain energy, a brain center is triggered—but orgasm happens exactly there in the brain, in the head.

That's why pornography has so much appeal, because pornography can directly stimulate your brain. Whether a woman is beautiful or ugly has nothing to do with your orgasm. An ugly woman can give you as beautiful an orgasm as a beautiful woman, but why don't you like the ugly woman? She does not appeal to your brain, that's all. Otherwise, as far as orgasm is concerned, both are equally capable. The ugliest woman or the most beautiful woman is immaterial—your head, your brain, is more interested in the form, in the beauty.

Tantra says once we understand this whole mechanism of orgasm, a greater understanding can arise.

One step more:

Modern research agrees up to this point—that orgasm happens in the brain. The woman's orgasm happens in the right side of the brain—about that, modern research is not yet capable of saying anything, but Tantra is. Tantra says the woman's orgasm happens in the right-side brain, because that is the feminine center. And the male orgasm happens in the left—that is the male side of the brain. Tantra goes further into this work and says that when these two sides of the brain come together great joy arises, total orgasm happens.

These two sides of the brain can come together easily—the less analytical you are, the closer they are. That's why an interpretative mind is never a happy mind. A non-interpretative mind is happier. Primitive people are more joyous than so-called civilized, educated, cultured people. Animals are happier than human beings; they don't have the analytical mind. The analytical mind makes the gap between the two sides of the brain bigger.

The more you think logically, the bigger is the gap between the two hemispheres of the brain. The less you think logically, the closer they come. The more poetic, the more esthetic your approach is, the more they will come close and the more possibility of joy, delight, and celebration there will be.

Finally, the last point, which I think will take many centuries for science to reach. The last point is that the joy is not happening exactly in the brain either—it happens in the witness who is standing behind both sides of the brain. If the witness is too attached to the male mind, then the joy will not be so great. Or, if the witness is attached too much to the female mind, then joy will be a little more, but still not so great.

Can't you see? Women are happier creatures than men. That's why they look more beautiful, more innocent, younger. They live longer and they live more peacefully, more contentedly. They are not worried as much; they don't commit suicide as often, they don't go mad as often. Men go mad twice as often as women. In suicide also, men outdo the women. And all the wars—if you include them as suicidal and murderous activities, then men have been doing nothing else! Down the centuries men have been preoccupied with preparing for war and killing people.

The feminine mind is more joyous because it is more poetic, more esthetic, more intuitive. But if you are not attached to any part and instead are just a witness, then your joy is utter, ultimate. This joy we have called in the East *anand*—bliss. To know this witness is to become one, absolutely one; then the woman and the man in you disappear completely, then they are lost into oneness.

Then to be orgasmic is your moment-to-moment existence. In that state, sex disappears automatically—because there is no need. When a person lives orgasmically twenty-four hours a day, what is the need for sex?

In your witnessing you become orgasmic. Orgasm then is not a momentary thing—then it is simply your nature. This is what ecstasy is.

the tantra vision
in practice

The Tantra vision is one of the greatest visions ever dreamt by humanity: a religion without a priest, a religion without a temple, a religion without an organization, a religion that does not destroy the individual but respects individuality tremendously, a religion that trusts in the ordinary man and woman. This trust goes very deep.

tantra trust

Tantra trusts in your body. No other religion trusts in your body. And when religions don't trust in your body, they create a split between you and your body. They make you an enemy of your body and they start destroying the wisdom of the body.

Tantra trusts in your body. Tantra trusts in your senses. Tantra trusts in your energy. Tantra trusts in you— *in toto*. Tantra does not deny anything, but transforms everything.

How to attain this Tantra vision?

This is the map to turn you on, and to turn you in, and to turn you beyond.

The first thing is the body. The body is your base, it is your ground, it is where you are grounded. To make you antagonistic toward the body is to destroy you, is to make you schizophrenic, is to make you miserable, is to create hell. You are the body. Of course, you are more than the body, but that "more" will follow later on. First you are the body. The body is your basic truth, so never be against your body. Whenever you are against the body, you are going against God. Whenever you are disrespectful to your body, you are losing contact with reality, because your body is your contact. Your body is your bridge. Your body is your temple. Tantra teaches reverence for the body, love, respect for the body, gratitude for the body. The body is marvelous. It is the greatest of mysteries.

But you have been taught to be against the body. So sometimes you are overwhelmed by the green tree, sometimes mystified by the moon and the sun, sometimes mystified by a flower. But you are never mystified by your own body. Your body is the most complex phenomenon in existence. No flower, no tree has such a beautiful body as you have. No moon, no sun, no star has such an evolved mechanism as you have.

But you have been taught to appreciate the flower, which is a simple thing. You have been taught to appreciate a tree, which is a simple thing. You have even been taught to appreciate stones, rocks, mountains, and rivers, but you have never been taught to respect your own body, to be mystified by it. Yes, it is very close, so it is easy to forget about it. It is obvious, so it is easy to neglect it. But it is the most beautiful phenomenon.

If you look at a flower, people will say "How esthetic!" And if you look at a woman's beautiful face or a man's beautiful face, people will say, "This is lust." If you go to a tree, and stand there, or look in a dazed state at the flower—your eyes wide open, your senses

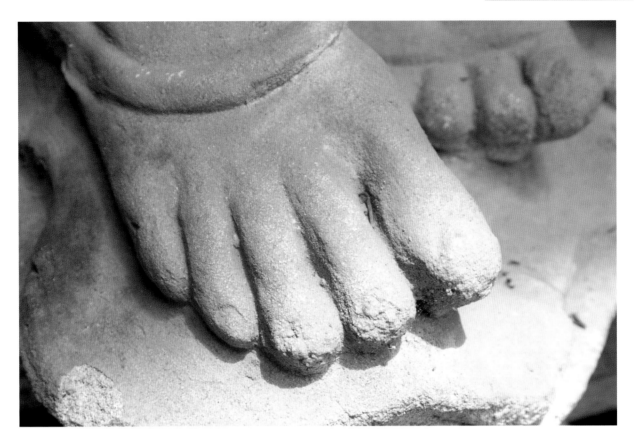

wide open to allow the beauty of the flower to enter you—people will think you are a poet or a painter or a mystic. But if you gaze on a woman or a man, just standing there with great reverence and respect, looking at the person with your eyes wide open and your senses drinking in the beauty, the police will catch hold of you! Nobody will say that you are a mystic or a poet, nobody will appreciate what you are doing. Something has gone wrong.

If you approach a stranger on the street and say, "What beautiful eyes you have!" you will feel embarrassed, he will feel embarrassed. He will not be able to say thank you to you. In fact, he will feel offended. He will feel offended, because who are you to interfere in his private life? Who are you to dare?

If you touch a tree, the tree feels happy. But if you touch a man, he will feel offended. What has gone wrong? Something has been damaged tremendously and deeply.

Tantra teaches you to reclaim respect for the body, love for the body. Tantra teaches you to look at the body as the greatest creation of existence. Tantra is the religion of the body. Of course it goes higher, but it never leaves the body; it is grounded there. It is the only religion that is really grounded in the earth: it has roots. Other religions are uprooted trees—dead, dull, dying; the juice does not flow in them.

Tantra is really juicy, very alive.

The first thing is to learn respect for the body, to unlearn all the nonsense that has been taught to you about the body. Otherwise, you

> *The body has to become weightless, so that you almost start walking above the earth—that is the Tantra way to walk.*

will never turn on, and you will never turn in, and you will never turn beyond. Start from the beginning. The body is your beginning.

The body has to be purified of many repressions. A great catharsis is needed for the body, a great purification. The body has become poisoned because you have been against it; you have repressed it in many ways. Your body is existing at the minimum, that's why you are miserable.

Tantra says: Bliss is possible only when you exist at the optimum—never before it. Bliss is possible only when you live intensely. How can you live intensely if you are against the body?

You are always lukewarm. The fire has cooled down. Down the centuries, the fire has been destroyed. The fire has to be rekindled. Tantra says: First purify the body—purify it of all repressions. Allow the body energy to flow, remove the blocks.

It is unusual to come across a person who has no blocks; it is unusual to come across a person whose body is not tight. Loosen this tightness—this tension is blocking your energy; the flow cannot be possible with this tension.

Why is everybody so uptight? Why can't they relax? Have you seen a cat sleeping, dozing in the afternoon? How simply and how beautifully the cat relaxes. Can't you relax the same way? You toss and turn, even in your bed you can't relax. The beauty of the cat's relaxation is that it relaxes utterly and yet is perfectly alert. A slight movement in the room and it will open its eyes, it will be ready to jump. It is not that it is just asleep—the cat's sleep is something to be learned—but people have forgotten how.

Tantra says: Learn from the cats—how they sleep, how they relax, how they live in a non-tense way. The whole animal world lives in that non-tense way. People have to learn this, because we have been conditioned wrongly. People have been programmed wrongly.

From childhood you have been programmed to be tight. You don't breathe... out of fear. Out of fear of sexuality, people don't breathe, because when you breathe deeply, your breath goes exactly to the sex center and hits it, massages it from the inside, excites it. Because you have been taught that sex is dangerous, each child starts breathing in a shallow way—hung up in the chest. They never go beyond that because if they go beyond it, suddenly, there is excitement: sexuality is aroused and fear arises. The moment you breathe deeply, sex energy is released.

Sex energy has to be released. It has to flow all over your being. Then your body will become orgasmic. But people are afraid to breathe, so afraid that almost half the lungs are full of carbon dioxide. That's why people are dull, that's why they don't look alert, that's why awareness is difficult.

It is not accidental that yoga and Tantra both teach deep breathing to unload the carbon dioxide from the lungs. The carbon dioxide is not for you—it has to be thrown out continuously, you have to breathe in new, fresh air, you have to breathe more oxygen. Oxygen will create your inner fire, oxygen will set you aflame. But oxygen will also inflame your sexuality. So only Tantra can allow truly deep breathing—even yoga cannot allow such deep breathing. Yoga also allows you to breathe in down to the navel—but not beyond that, not to cross the hara center, not to cross svadhisthan, because once you cross svadhisthan you jump into the muladhar.

Only Tantra allows you total being and total flow. Tantra gives you unconditional freedom, whatsoever you are and whatsoever you can be. Tantra puts no boundaries on you; it does not define you, it simply gives you total freedom. The understanding is that when you are totally free, then much is possible.

This has been my observation: people who are sexually repressed become unintelligent. Only very sexually alive people are intelligent people. Now, the idea that sex is sin must have damaged intelligence—must have damaged it badly. When you are really flowing and your sexuality has neither fight nor conflict with you, when you cooperate with it, your mind will function at its optimum. You will be intelligent, alert, alive.

The body has to be befriended, says Tantra.

Do you touch your own body sometimes? Do you ever feel your own body, or do you remain as if you were encased in a dead thing? That's what is happening. People are almost frozen; they are carrying the body like a casket. It is heavy, it obstructs, it does not help you to communicate with reality. If you allow the electricity of the body flow to move from the

> *Find new ways to explore the other. Don't get fixed in routines. All routines are anti-life: routines are in the service of death. You can always invent—there is no limit to inventions.*

toe to the head, if you allow total freedom for its energy—the bioenergy—you will become a river and you will not feel the body at all. You will feel almost bodiless. Not fighting with the body, you become bodiless. Fighting with the body, the body becomes a burden. And carrying your body as a burden you can never fly into the sky.

The body has to become weightless, so that you almost start walking above the earth—that is the Tantra way to walk. You are so weightless that there is no gravitation—you can simply fly. But that comes out of great acceptance. It is going to be difficult to accept your body. You condemn it, you always find fault with it. You never appreciate it, you never love it, and then you want a miracle: that somebody will come along and love your body. If you yourself cannot love it, then how are you going to find somebody else to love your body? If you yourself cannot love it, nobody else is going to love your body, because your vibe will repel people.

You fall in love with a person who loves himself, never otherwise. The first love has to be toward oneself—only from that center can other kinds of love arise. You don't love your body. You hide it in a thousand and one ways. You

> *The beauty of tears, the beauty of laughter; the poetry of tears, and the poetry of laughter are available to humans only.*

hide your body's smell, you hide your body's shape in clothes, you hide yourself in ornamentation. You try to create some beauty that you continuously feel you are missing, and in that very effort you become artificial.

Do you ever come across a bird that is ugly? Do you ever come across a deer that is ugly? It never happens. They don't go to any beauty parlors, and they don't consult any experts. They simply accept themselves and they are beautiful in their acceptance. In that very acceptance they shower beauty upon themselves.

The moment you accept yourself you become beautiful. When you are delighted with your own body, you will delight others also. Many people will fall in love with you, because you yourself are in love with yourself. When you are angry with yourself, you know that you are ugly, you know that you are repulsive, horrible. This idea will repel people; this idea will not help them to fall in love with you, it will keep them away. Even if they were coming closer to you, the moment they feel your vibration, they will move away.

There is no need to chase anybody. The chasing game arises only because we have not been in love with ourselves. Otherwise, people come to you. It becomes almost impossible for them not to fall in love with you if you are in love with yourself.

Why did so many people come to Buddha and why did so many people come to Saraha and why did so many people come to Jesus? These people were in love with themselves. They were in such great love and they were so delighted with their being that it was natural for whosoever would pass to be pulled by them;

like magnets they pulled people. They were so enchanted with their own being, how could you avoid that enchantment? Just being there was a great bliss.

Tantra teaches the first thing: Be loving toward your body, befriend your body, revere your body, respect your body, take care of your body—it is nature's gift. Treat it well and it will reveal great mysteries to you. All growth depends on how you are related to your body.

The second thing Tantra speaks about is the senses. The senses are your doors of perception, the senses are your windows into reality. What is your eyesight? What are your ears? What is your nose? Windows into reality, windows into existence. If you see rightly, you will see God everywhere. The eyes are not to be closed, the eyes have to be opened rightly. The eyes are not to be destroyed. The ears are not to be destroyed because all these sounds are divine.

The birds are chanting mantras and the trees are giving sermons in silence. All sounds are divine, and all forms are divine. If you don't have sensitivity in you, how will you know the divine? You go to a church or to a temple to find God… yet godliness is all over the place! In a man-made temple, in a man-made church, you go to find God? Why? God is everywhere, alive and kicking everywhere. But for that you need clean senses, purified senses.

Tantra teaches that the senses are the doors of perception. The doors have been dulled. You have to drop that dullness and your senses have to be cleansed. Your senses are like a mirror that has become dull because so much dust has gathered upon it. The dust has to be cleaned away.

Look at the Tantra approach to everything. Taste God in every taste. Flow totally into your touch, because whatsoever you touch is divine. It is a total reversal of the ascetic, so-called religions. It is a radical revolution—from the very roots.

Touch, smell, taste, see, and hear as totally as possible. You will have to learn the language because society has deceived you; it has made you forget.

Every child is born with beautiful senses. Watch a child. When he looks at something, he is completely absorbed. When he is playing with his toys, he is utterly absorbed. When he looks, he becomes just the eyes. Look at the eyes of a child. When he hears, he becomes just the ears. When he eats something, he is just there on the tongue. He becomes just the taste. See a child eating an apple. With what gusto! With what great energy! With what delight! See a child running after a butterfly in the garden… so absorbed that even if God were available, he would not run that way. Such a tremendous, meditative state—and without any effort. See a child collecting seashells on the beach as if he were collecting diamonds. Everything is precious when the senses are alive. Everything is clear when the senses are alive.

Later on in life, the same child will look at reality as if hidden behind a darkened glass. Much smoke and dust have gathered on the glass, and you are hidden behind it and you are looking. Because of this, everything looks dull and dead. You look at the tree and the tree looks dull because your eyes are dull. You hear a song, but there is no appeal in it because your ears are dull. You can hear a Saraha and you will

" Go to the river and let the river flow through your hands. Feel it! Swim and feel the water again as the fish feels it. Don't miss an opportunity to revive your senses. "

you and comes too close, you start moving backward. We protect our territory. We don't touch and we don't allow others to touch; we don't hold hands, we don't hug. We don't enjoy each other's being.

Go to the tree and touch the tree. Touch the rock. Go to the river and let the river flow through your hands. Feel it! Swim, and feel the water again as the fish feels it. Don't miss any opportunity to revive your senses. There are a thousand and one opportunities the whole day. There is no need to make separate time for it. The whole day is a training in sensitivity. Use all the opportunities.

Standing under your shower, use the opportunity—feel the touch of the water falling on you. Lie down on the ground, naked, feel the earth. Lie down on the beach, feel the sand. Listen to the sounds of the sand, listen to the sounds of the sea. Use every opportunity—only then will you be able to learn the language of the senses again. Tantra can be understood only when your body is alive and your senses feel.

Free your senses from habits. Habits are one of the root causes of dullness. Find out new ways of doing things. Invent new ways of loving.

I have heard:

The doctor told the working chap that he could not complete his examination without a sample of urine. The small boy who was sent with the specimen spilled most of it while messing around. Fearing a good beating, he topped it off with a bit more urine from a cow in the field.

The doctor hastily sent for the man, who returned home to his wife in a furious temper

not be able to appreciate him, because your intelligence is dull.

Reclaim your forgotten language. Whenever you have time, be more in your senses. Eating—don't just eat, try to learn the forgotten language of taste again. Touch the bread, feel the texture of it. Feel with open eyes, feel with closed eyes. While chewing, chew it—you are chewing God. Remember it! It will be disrespectful not to chew well, not to taste well. Let it be a prayer, and you will start the rising of a new consciousness in you. You will learn the way of Tantra alchemy.

Touch people more. We have become very touchy about touch. If somebody is talking to *and said, "That's you and your fancy positions! You would be on top, wouldn't you? And now I am going to have a baby!"*

People have fixed habits. Even while making love they often make it in the same position, "the missionary posture."

Find new ways of feeling. Each experience has to be created with great sensitivity. When you make love, make it a great celebration. Each time, bring some new creativity into it. Sometimes dance before you make love. Sometimes pray before you make love. Sometimes go running into the forest, and then make love. Sometimes go swimming and then make love. Then each love experience will create more and more sensitivity in you and it will never become dull and boring.

Find out new ways to explore the other. Don't get fixed in routines. All routines are anti-life: routines are in the service of death. You can always invent—there is no limit to inventions. Sometimes a small change will tremendously benefit you. If you always eat at the table, sometimes go out to the lawn—sit on the lawn and eat there. You will be surprised: it is a totally different experience. The smell of the freshly-cut grass, the birds hopping around and singing, the fresh air, the sunrays, and the feel of the grass underneath. It cannot be the same experience as when you sit on a chair and eat at your table; it is a totally different experience—all the ingredients are different.

Some time try just eating naked and you will be surprised. Just a small change—nothing much, you are sitting naked—but you will have a totally different experience because something new has been added to it. If you eat with a spoon and fork, eat sometimes with bare hands and you will have a different experience; your touch will bring new warmth to the food. A spoon is a dead thing: when you eat with a spoon or a fork, you are far away. It is that same fear of touching anything—even food cannot be touched. You will miss the texture, the touch, the feel of it. The food has as much feel as it has taste.

Many experiments have been done in the West on the fact that when we are enjoying anything, there are many things we are not aware of that contribute to the experience. For example, close your eyes and hold your nose and then eat an onion. Tell somebody to give it to you when you don't know what he is giving— whether he is giving you an onion or an apple. It will be difficult for you to make out the difference if your nose is completely closed and your eyes are closed. It will be impossible for you to decide whether it is an onion or an apple, because the taste is not only taste; fifty percent of it comes from the nose, and much comes from the eyes. It is not just taste; all the senses contribute. When you eat with your hands, your touch is contributing. It will be more tasty. It will be more human, more natural.

Find new ways in everything. Let that be one of your disciplines. Tantra says: If you can continue finding new ways every day, your life will remain a thrill, an adventure. You will never be bored. You will always be curious to know, you will always be on the verge of seeking the unknown and the unfamiliar. Your eyes will remain clear and your senses will remain clear, because when you are always on the verge of seeking, exploring, finding, searching, you cannot become dull, you cannot become stupid.

> *Look at the Tantra approach to everything. Flow totally into your touch, because whatsoever you touch is divine...Touch, smell, taste, see, and hear as totally as possible.*

Psychologists say that by the age of seven, stupidity starts. It initially starts about the age of four, but by the seventh year it is very apparent. Children start becoming dull by the age of seven.

In fact, the child learns fifty percent of all the learnings of his whole life by the time he is seven. If he lives to seventy, in the remaining sixty-three years, he will learn only fifty percent—fifty percent he has already learned. What happens? He becomes dull; he stops learning. If you think in terms of intelligence, by the age of seven a child starts becoming old. Physically he will become old later on—from the age of thirty-five he will start declining—but mentally he is already on the decline.

You will be surprised that the average mental age is twelve. People don't often grow beyond that; they are stuck there. That's why you see so much childishness in the world. Insult a person who is sixty years of age, and within seconds he is just a twelve-year-old child. He will behave in such a way that you will not believe that a grownup could be so childish.

People are always ready to fall back. Their mental age is just skin-deep, hidden behind. Just scratch a little, and their mental age comes out. Their physical age is not of much importance.

Most people die childish; they never grow.

Tantra says: Learn new ways of doing things and free yourself of habits as much as possible. Tantra says: Don't be imitative; otherwise, your senses will become dull. Find out ways of doing things in your own way. Have your signature on everything that you do.

Just the other night a woman was telling me that the love between her and her husband has disappeared. Now they are staying together just for the children. I told her to meditate, to be friendly to the husband. If love has disappeared, all has not disappeared; friendship is still possible. Be friendly. And she said, "It is difficult. When a cup is broken, it is broken."

I told her that it seemed she had not heard that Zen people in Japan will first purchase a cup from the supermarket, bring it home, break it, then glue it together again to make it individual and special. Otherwise, it is just a marketplace thing. And if a friend comes to visit and you give him tea in an ordinary cup and saucer, that is not good; that is ugly, that is not respectful. So they will bring a fresh new cup and break it. Of course, then there is no other cup in the world exactly like it—there cannot be. Glued together, now it has some individuality, a signature. And when Zen people go to each other's house or each other's monastery, they will not just sip the tea. First they will appreciate the cup, they will look at it. The way it has been joined together is a work of art—the way the pieces have been broken and put together again. The woman

understood and she started laughing. She said,
"Then it is possible."

Bring individuality to things. To imitate is to
miss life. To be imitative is to be neurotic. The
only way to be sane in the world is to be individual,
authentically individual. Be your own being.

So first, the body has to be purified of
repressions. Second, the senses have to be
made alive again. Third, the mind has to drop
neurotic thinking, obsessive thinking, and it has
to learn ways of silence.

Whenever it is possible, relax. Whenever it
is possible, put the mind aside. Now you will
say, "That is easy to say, but how to put the mind
aside? It goes on and on." There is a way.

Tantra says, Watch these three awarenesses:

Awareness one: let the mind go, let the mind
be filled with thoughts, and simply watch,
detached. There is no need to be worried about
it—just watch. Just be the observer, and by and
by you will see that silent gaps have started
coming to you.

Then, awareness two: when you have
become aware that gaps have started coming,
then become aware of the watcher. Now watch
the watcher and new gaps will start coming—
the watcher will start disappearing, just like the
thoughts. One day, the thinker also starts
disappearing. Then real silence arises.

With the third awareness, both object and
subject are gone and you have entered into
the beyond.

When these three things are attained—
body purified of repressions, senses freed from
dullness, and mind liberated from obsessive
thinking—a vision arises in you free from all
illusion. That is the Tantra vision.

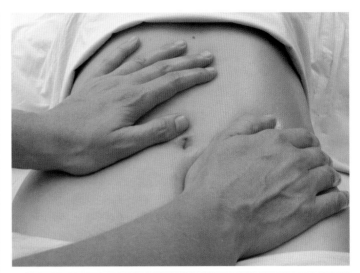

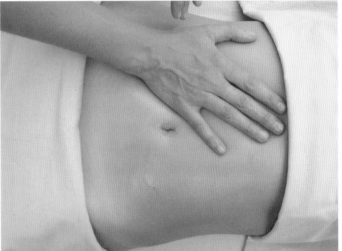

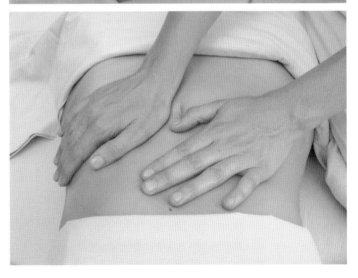

about the author

Osho (1931–1990) is a contemporary mystic whose teachings have inspired millions of people from all walks of life. His works, which are published in more than 40 languages, are transcribed from extemporaneous talks given over a period of 35 years. They cover everything from the individual search for happiness to the most pressing social, political, and spiritual concerns of our time. *The Sunday Times* of London has named Osho as one of the "1000 Makers of the 20th Century." His books are best-sellers in many languages and many countries. Other books by Osho on Tantra include:

The Book of Secrets

Tantra, Spirituality and Sex

Tantra: The Supreme Understanding

The Tantra Experience (previously *The Tantra Vision*, vol. 1)

Tantric Transformation (previously *The Tantra Vision*, vol. 2)

Meditation: The First and Last Freedom—A Practical Guide to Meditation

For the availability of editions in different languages, please check the Osho website.

"He quotes Jesus, Buddha, Mahavira, Lao Tzu, Sufis, and old Zen masters with stupendous memory, interpreting them with a freshness and directness as if they were speaking today, as if they wore jeans."

Die Zeit, Germany

"Osho is one of the most remarkable orators I have ever heard."

BERNARD LEVIN, *The Times*, UK

OSHO INTERNATIONAL WEBSITE

For more information see: www.osho.com—a comprehensive website in several languages with information about the author, his work, and the Osho International Meditation Resort.